D1282219

Shifting the Monkey

Todd Whitaker

Solution Tree | Press

The art of protecting GOOD PEOPLE from
LIARS, CRIERS, and OTHER SLACKERS

Shifting

the

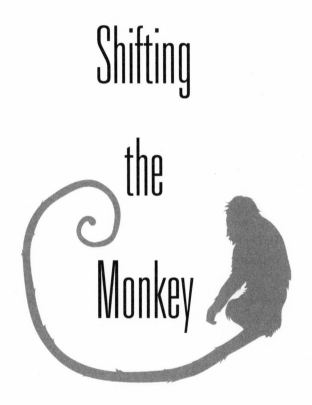

Monkey

Todd
Whitaker

Solution Tree | Press

Copyright © 2012 by Solution Tree Press (Originally
published by Triple Nickel Press, a wholly owned subsidary of
Solution Tree)

All rights reserved, including the right of reproduction of this
book in whole or in part in any form.

555 North Morton Street
Bloomington, IN 47404
800.733.6786
FAX: 812.336.7790

email: info@solution-tree.com
solution-tree.com

Printed in the United States of America

Library of Congress Cataloging-in-Publication Data
Whitaker, Todd, 1959-
  Shifting the monkey : the art of protecting good people from
liars, criers, and other slackers / by Todd Whitaker.
      pages cm
  Includes bibliographical references and index.
  ISBN 978-1-936763-08-5 (hardcover with dustjacket) 1.
Problem employees. 2. Performance standards. 3. Personnel
management. 4. Corporate culture. I. Title.
  HF5549.5.E42W484 2014
  658.3'145--dc23
                                              2014001673

Table of Contents

Chapter 5

Chapter 6

Chapter 7

Epilogue

Chapter 1

It's a Jungle Out There

Don't you hate it when . . .

- Certain workers get away with shirking their responsibilities and even intimidating other employees?

- Management issues strict new rules and regulations that make life miserable for everyone, just because of a few goof-offs?

- Big signs in stores warn against shoplifting or breaking items, with such stern language that you feel uncomfortable just being in the store?

- You have to keep punching the answers to questions and sequences of numbers into the telephone when you're calling a company, only to have the person who finally gets on the phone ask you the same questions and insist that you repeat the same numbers?

These are just a few examples of how misguided leadership can damage a workplace, alienate customers, and otherwise make life annoying, even miserable, for lots of people.

Lately, these problems seem to be getting worse. Lots of ideas for dealing with them have been proposed over the years, but the "solutions" vanish as quickly as they arise because they miss the real issue, which is simple: monkeys are out of place. They've shifted to the wrong people's backs.

Warning: The monkeys I'm talking about aren't the cute, fun furry creatures you see in zoos. The monkeys I'm referring to are the responsibilities, obligations, and problems everyone deals with every day. They can be distracting, annoying, cumbersome, and pretty stinky! You can't avoid them; they are part of work and life.

You can easily handle your fair share of normal monkeys, as long as you feel valued and supported. But you can just as easily become overwhelmed when you get stuck shouldering other people's inappropriate monkeys. Some monkeys simply shouldn't be your problem. Anger Monkeys, Guilt Monkeys, and Attack Monkeys are just a few of the monkeys people use to shift their burdens to others. And when they do, monkeys start to pile up—on other people's backs. Every so often, someone like you—someone who works hard and cares about the organization—looks around and notices that other people aren't so burdened. You start to wonder, "Why do I have to carry their load, too?" You get resentful. You might even feel like there's no point trying hard anymore because no matter what you do, the monkeys on your back keep multiplying.

Think of an employee—and you probably know one—who performs poorly yet complains loudly. There's a very good chance his manager will reassign some of his duties, thinking, "This guy's not going to do it right anyway, so I might as well have someone else take care of it." The manager was right in thinking that the employee won't do the job correctly, but wrong in assigning the task to someone else—someone who now has a monkey she doesn't deserve. The monkey has been shifted.

Monkeys are the responsibilities, obligations, and problems everyone deals with every day. You can easily handle your share of normal monkeys, but you can just as easily become overwhelmed when you get stuck shouldering other people's inappropriate monkeys.

How about the angry customer who harangues an unfortunate department store clerk, demanding this and that, letting everyone within earshot know exactly what's wrong with this crummy place? That customer creates a Discomfort Monkey, which lands squarely on the back of the poor clerk and any customers nearby.

Then there's the boss who, eager to impress the higher-ups, forces all her employees to really push the "premium membership" on every single customer—even those who obviously don't want it, who clearly resent being pressured to pay for something they don't want, and who make their resentment well known. Now you've got monkeys on the backs of angry customers as well as hapless employees.

Poorly performing employees, angry customers, and clueless bosses are shifting a lot of monkeys, taking advantage of the dedicated, mature, caring people who are forced to carry those monkeys and ignoring their superhuman efforts. Yikes! It almost makes you want to stop being good or nice. Shouldn't lazy workers be expected to do their fair share, nasty customers to mend their ways, and misguided bosses to wise up? Aren't they getting a weird kind of reward for their bad behavior?

Why Slackers Go Monkey-Free

It's a sad fact in today's world that negative, poorly performing people tend to get a disproportionate amount of power, attention, and empathy. They continue to behave obnoxiously and unfairly because they're rewarded for doing so. Slacker employees are given less work. Rude customers get immediate attention and endless attempts to placate them. Program-pushing bosses are praised for meeting quotas.

> Negative, poorly performing people tend to get a disproportionate amount of power, attention, and empathy. They continue to behave obnoxiously and unfairly because they're rewarded for doing so.

This even happens when a crime occurs. Think about it: the perpetrator is rewarded with much more attention than the victim, and the press and law enforcement officials very carefully use the word *alleged* for fear of unfairly incriminating the suspect. Yet any sordid rumors about the victim will immediately become headline news splashed all over *Entertainment Tonight*!

You can be sure that negative people don't have any monkeys on *their* backs. They don't feel the least bit bad about being slackers or jerks. Why should they, when the rest of us carry their monkeys? It's we who are unhappy, uncomfortable, put out, over-worked, frustrated, fearful, and angry. We know the situation is wrong and unfair, but we feel there is nothing we can do to change it.

How to Put Monkeys in Their Place

Fortunately, monkey business doesn't have to be business as usual. I'm going to show how you, as a leader at work and in other aspects of your life, can shift out-of-place monkeys off the backs of the good, hardworking people and onto the backs of the poorly performing, badly behaved people, where they belong. Shifting the monkey may sound like a zookeeper's technique, but it's actually a powerful way to look at leading and living.

By the way, you may have noticed that I often use the terms *good* and *bad* when referring to people. For the purposes of this book, *good* means honest people who try hard, are responsible, and cooperate with others for the benefit of the whole—in other words, the vast majority of people. *Bad* means the opposite: dishonest people who are lazy, unreliable, and self-centered.

I'll show you how to shift the monkey by improving your leadership skills. Don't worry; it won't require mastering complicated technical details or earning advanced degrees. It's simply a matter of changing your thought patterns. Instead of wondering, "How do I protect myself?"—which allows monkeys to start shifting around—a great leader asks, "How do I protect my good people? How do I make the world a better place?" In so doing, the leader ensures that monkeys stay right where they belong.

> Instead of wondering, "How do I protect myself?" a great leader asks, "How do I protect my good people? How do I make the world a better place?"

You won't be able to "fix" people or magically change the world. But you *will* go a long way toward making sure that good people aren't saddled with monkeys that don't belong to them and that bad people are forced to carry their own monkeys. When it comes to liars, criers, and other slackers, you may not change their minds or attitudes, but you *can* change their behavior by becoming a better leader.

And that's what really matters.

Chapter 2

Out-of-Place Monkeys

et's follow Jim, a branch manager in a cable TV company who oversees the work of about thirty people. Jim dreads interacting with his employees because it seems that every time he does, he winds up taking on some of their duties.

One morning, the cable installers told him they had to cancel three installations because they didn't know how to deal with very old fuse boxes. Jim handled the problem by calling the installation specialist at company headquarters. Since Jim was not a technician, he had to spend a long time going over the installers' information to make sure he got it right and could explain it to the installers. The installers had additional questions, so Jim made four more follow-up calls to the specialist.

Obviously, it would have been much more efficient for the installers to call the specialist or study the detailed installation manuals the company had carefully prepared. Meanwhile, Jim took time away from his own duties, and the installers lost time making second trips to the three cancelled installations. Plus, three very unhappy customers told all their friends about the miserable service they received.

The very same day, financial officer Heather cornered Jim in the hallway and announced that she couldn't complete the expense projections until she had certain data. With a sigh, Jim said he would look into it. More work for Jim, while Heather simply waited for him to get the data. She could have gotten the information herself if she'd had the initiative or if Jim had declined to take on her duties. "But why should I," she figured, "when he'll do it for me?"

Later that day, Jim rifled through a stack of customer complaint emails and phone messages. Every complaint needed a response. Two employees, Greg and Melanie, were officially assigned to handle complaints, but Jim handed the entire stack to Greg, who was particularly adept with customers. He didn't even bother asking Melanie, because she was slow and argumentative. Instead, he decided she would spend the day "filing"—actually, she would spend the day goofing off, because there wasn't much filing to do. Jim leans heavily on Greg and worries sometimes that he will rebel or quit because he's fed up with having to do the bulk of the work. But he figures he'll cross that bridge when he comes to it.

In this situation, where are the monkeys? They are on Jim's back, Greg's back, and the back of the tech guy who shouldn't have had to spend extra time explaining things nicely and simply to Jim. There are also monkeys on the backs of the angry customers who don't get the service they're promised.

Where should the monkeys be? On the backs of the installers, Heather, and Melanie, who all should have done their jobs.

Jim has a major problem with out-of-place monkeys. And it's not just Jim: out-of-place monkeys are running rampant in all sorts of businesses, from major international corporations to little Mom 'n' Pop sandwich shops. They're on the backs of white collar and blue collar folks alike. Out-of-place monkeys can destroy a shop, company branch, department, or an entire business, and can cause any hairs a manager hasn't already torn out of his head to turn gray.

It doesn't have to be that way. These monkeys can be corralled and controlled by changing the behavior of certain employees.

Out-of-place monkeys are running rampant in all sorts of businesses, from major international corporations to little Mom 'n' Pop sandwich shops.

When Are Monkeys Acceptable?

Monkeys—whether big or small, routine or unusual —are facts of life in the business world; they pop up all the time. Dealing with monkeys is a routine part of any job, especially when you're a manager. (Monkeys are actually a good thing for a manager, because without them, he'd be out of a job!)

At a bank, for example, monkeys can take the form of unhappy customers, tellers who can't balance their accounts, ATMs that are on the blink, and so on. At a factory's maintenance and repair facility, monkeys can appear as an overload of work requests, too few repair technicians, and a lack of proper tools. In a restaurant, the monkeys may include shortages of a certain food item in the middle of lunch rush, a stove that burns too hot, too few waiters, or bugs in the kitchen. In every case, it's the manager's job to ensure all of these monkeys are handled effectively and efficiently by the designated employees.

So monkeys are absolutely normal and not a concern in a well-led business. The trouble begins when the monkeys are not where they should be and some people are forced to do more work to make up for others who aren't doing their jobs. All of the work may still get done, but there's a risk that the good workers will become resentful or quit—or adopt the same lazy habits that seem to work so well for the slackers.

> Monkeys are absolutely normal and not a concern in a well-led business. The trouble begins when the monkeys are not where they should be.

When employees' monkeys are piled onto the manager's back, the result can be chaos as the manager tries to handle other people's problems instead of doing her job—which is to manage.

Why Do Monkeys Keep Shifting?

Can we blame all monkey-shifting on incompetent or lazy workers who can't or won't do their jobs? Not necessarily. That's where it begins, because procrastination and sloth cause the monkeys to pile up. But at that point, the monkeys are still on the backs of the right people.

Things start to get out of hand when these employees are allowed to shift their monkeys to someone else. This happens when the manager reassigns duties to other, more competent employees; when a lazy employee persuades or bullies a coworker into taking on some of his work; when a good employee just goes ahead and does the work without being asked, for the benefit of the company; or when a manager volunteers to take up the slack, just to keep the department humming along. Sometimes just a portion of the work is shifted—say, something as "harmless" as calling the headquarters technician on behalf of the installers. But no matter how large or small the duty (or monkey) may be, it has been shifted.

Any small shift signals the beginning of big trouble, because once poor performers know they can shift their monkeys, they will keep doing it. Productivity will suffer, and the good employees will become increasingly resentful, disengaged, and otherwise disgruntled. The manager will become, in effect, just another employee, and upper management will become concerned because the manager isn't doing his work and his employees aren't doing theirs.

> Once poor performers know they can shift their monkeys, they will keep doing it.

In short, the monkey problem is not lazy or incompetent employees who aren't doing their work or are trying to get others to do it for them. The problem is that they have *been allowed to succeed* in shifting their monkeys.

Why Do Millions of Managers Struggle With Monkeys?

The major reason managers become overwhelmed with out-of-place monkeys is this: they think it's easier to take monkeys off the backs of poorly performing employees than it is to encourage or force those employees to handle their own responsibilities. In fact, some managers may have no idea what it's like to *not* be surrounded by a troop of screeching, jumping monkeys; monkey business is business as usual for them.

So when an employee points to a monkey—perhaps by asking something seemingly innocuous like, "How do I handle this?" or "Can you help me?"—the manager reacts automatically by shifting part or all of the monkey to his own back. He thinks that's the best choice. But even if the manager takes on just a small portion of the situation or responsibility, that monkey cannot be tamed and sent on its way until the manager does *something*. The task might be reviewing certain numbers, conferring with someone, getting another staff member to write a report, or even just thinking about the problem. Whatever the task is, the monkey will stay on the manager's back until he does whatever needs to be done. Meanwhile, the lazy employee is happy because she doesn't have to do anything but wait around for an answer from the boss.

This kind of monkey-shifting can happen in a thousand different ways, some subtle and some obvious. For example, the employee says, "Boss, the shipment is late," and the manager replies, "I'll look into it." Where's the monkey now? On the manager's back.

The employee says, "Boss, I don't know if I should increase or decrease the allotment on the Jones account," and the manager answers, "I'll crunch some numbers." Where's the monkey now? On the manager's back.

Even if the manager takes on just a small portion of the responsibility, that monkey cannot be tamed and sent on its way until the manager does *something*.

The employee says, "Boss, I don't know how to do this," and the manager instantly offers to do the necessary research. Where's the monkey now? On the manager's back.

These indirect questions about the late shipment, the Jones allotment, or how to do something are all monkeys that should be calmed, groomed, and sent on their way—*by the employees themselves*. Instead, these monkeys are invited (or, more accurately, forced) to move into the manager's office until the manager gets around to doing what the employees were supposed to do. As they multiply, the monkeys become more unruly and difficult. First one monkey, then five, ten, twenty, or maybe even fifty! No wonder so many managers end up taking work home or coming in on the weekends.

Loaded down with other people's monkeys, there's no way a manager can do the real work of managing a department and communicating with the rest of the company. He's become a zookeeper frantically trying to keep his ever-growing menagerie under control. If the day ends without a major problem due to monkeys escaping and running rampant through the department, he considers it a great day.

> Loaded down with other people's monkeys, there's no way a manager can do the real work of managing a department and communicating with the rest of the company.

The Rise of the Monkey

The concept of out-of-place monkeys was introduced by William Oncken, Jr., and Donald Wass in their 1974 *Harvard Business Review* article titled "Management Time: Who's Got the Monkey?" It was written at a time when companies, especially large ones, gave their workers very little autonomy. This practically forced employees to shift monkeys to their supervisors, the only people allowed to make decisions.

Oncken and Wass set the stage for their concept by noting that every manager has to chunk his time into segments that they called boss-imposed time, system-imposed time, self-imposed time, subordinate-imposed time, and discretionary time. These fairly self-explanatory segments are each devoted to meeting the needs of different stakeholders in the organization—except for discretionary time.

Ideally, managers would spend their discretionary time thinking up ways to improve the department's performance (and their own chances for advancement). Unfortunately, handling out-of-place monkeys and their repercussions usually eats up that vital time. To protect discretionary time, Oncken and

Wass offered two rules for dealing with monkeys: (1) either feed them or shoot them, and (2) keep the monkey population below the number you have time to tend.

While this concept made sense back then, it was completely boss-centered. This monkey-reduction plan was designed to help the leader protect *himself* by freeing up his time and deflecting responsibility and extra work. It was for managers interested in survival.

A New Look at Leadership

Oncken and Wass had a great insight in the monkey concept, but things have changed; management no longer keeps such a tight rein on everyone's behavior. Their ideas were geared for what I call Tier One leaders, who are primarily interested in shielding themselves. Managers certainly want to guard against being overwhelmed with other people's responsibilities; if managers don't have time for their own duties, the entire department or organization will suffer. But operating as a Tier One leader isn't enough today.

Tier Two leaders go beyond; they protect their good people as well as themselves. These leaders recognize that their good workers are more at risk than they are. The workers are on the frontlines, after all.

Think about a restaurant: the manager can sit in her office, but the wait staff and maître d' must deal with the customers. The manager can even avoid the employees most of the time by keeping her door locked and ignoring them. She doesn't have to deal with workplace bullies, either, as they typically don't bully superiors.

In an office with one manager and three secretaries, one of whom is a bullying male, you can be pretty sure he's bullying the other two secretaries, not the boss. And if he *is* pushing the boss around, just imagine what he's doing to the powerless secretaries who are at his mercy all day long!

The best leaders are Tier Three leaders, who go way beyond protecting themselves and others; they look for ways to ensure things are *always* going well, even when they're not present. They shift monkeys to change behavior, so that people behave themselves even when the boss isn't looking. These leaders make sure their good workers are always protected, feel rewarded, and have autonomy. This makes a great deal of sense, because if you don't take good care of your good waiters, you won't have a restaurant to manage; if you don't take care of your good salespeople, you won't have a business anymore; and if you don't take care of your customers, they'll go elsewhere.

> Tier Three leaders look for ways to ensure things are *always* going well, even when they're not present.

Here's a simple way to view the leadership tiers:

- Tier One—The self-focused leader who goes in the back office and closes the door

- Tier Two—The team-focused leader who goes out front periodically to make sure the mean employees aren't abusing the others

- Tier Three—The organization-focused leader who shifts the monkey back to the ineffectual people so they won't behave badly again, whether the leader is checking or not

Three Important Questions

As I travel around the country speaking to business groups, people tell me they understand the difference between normal monkeys and out-of-place monkeys. The monkey concept is very easy to understand—but it's hard to put into practice.

People ask me, "So how *should* I respond when an employee says, 'Boss, the shipment is late,' or 'I don't know if I should increase or decrease the allotment on the Jones account,' or 'My numbers don't add up'?"

They want to know where the fine line is between being helpful and being a pushover, and how you make sure you stay monkey-free. They worry that it's not wise to keep saying no when staff members ask for help—especially when the easiest way to handle the problem is to do it yourself or when the person asking is the least likely to succeed. How do you keep up morale when you're saying no to monkeys all day long? Don't you have to say yes once in a while?

These are good questions, and to answer them you must learn to see things in a new way. You must keep asking yourself the following new questions:

1. Where is the monkey?
2. Where should the monkey be?
3. How do I shift the monkey to its proper place?

We'll talk more about the first two questions in the next chapter, and then spend a couple chapters looking at ways to shift the monkey back where it belongs. You'll learn that the key techniques are to treat everyone well, make decisions based on your best people, and protect yourself *after* you protect your people. There are times when it's OK to say yes to the monkey, as we'll see in chapter 6, but usually, it's in everyone's best interest to make sure monkeys stay put.

This is a business book, so I'll be talking a lot about the workplace, but the truth is we're constantly dealing with out-of-place monkeys in family life, at the grocery store, the Little League game, the movie theatre—everywhere. You're a leader in many areas, and you can apply everything you read here to other arenas of your life.

Always remember:

* Monkeys are a normal part of business and the rest of life.

* The real problems start when monkeys shift to the backs of the wrong people, people who must exert extra effort and are likely to become overwhelmed and resentful.

* Managers are often unaware of the problem because they're used to seeing some employees shirk their responsibilities and used to picking up those monkeys for them.

* The monkey concept was introduced in the 1970s in the context of teaching managers how to protect themselves. Protecting yourself may be necessary, but it's only Tier One leadership.

* We should go beyond shielding ourselves and learn how to ensure that our good people are protected and that things are *always* going well, even when we're not looking. That's Tier Three leadership.

* Keep asking yourself the three important questions: Where is the monkey? Where should the
  monkey be? How do I shift the monkey to its
  proper place?

Chapter 3

Where Is the Monkey, and Where Should It Be?

1. Where is the monkey?
2. Where should the monkey be?
3. How do I shift the monkey to its proper place?

Have you ever gone to a store checkout stand, laid your items on the counter, and handed the clerk a twenty-dollar bill—only to watch her whip out a special pen, mark the bill, and hold it up to the light to see if it's fake? I don't know about you, but I feel defenseless when this happens. The only thing I can do is to take out my own pen and mark the change that the clerk gives back to me. Then I bite the coins to see if they are real.

Checking money happens a lot these days, but it is truly amazing when the clerk knows you. She might even smile and say, "Hi, good to see you again!"—as she then takes out that pen to mark your twenty. It's enough to make you wonder if you look like a counterfeiter, with ink stains on your fingers and a guilty look on your face.

Don't worry, you don't. What's happened is that the store has decided to treat everyone as potential criminals. Every bill larger than a ten gets the pen treatment, no matter who presents it, no matter how often—if ever—a counterfeit has been discovered. This common practice is a good example of how management can become so worried about protecting the organization that it risks offending all honest customers. In this situation, where is the monkey?

It might be on the back of the clerk, if customers give her trouble over the bill checking. It is certainly on the backs of the customers, who could be offended by the suggestion that they are counterfeiters or worried that they might be unknowingly passing phony money. How many customers were affected? The company will never know. What they *will* know is that some customers just don't come back again.

Constantly Check for Monkeys

As a leader, it's your job to check for monkeys in every situation, even the smallest interactions.

Imagine that you're about to conduct a big meeting that requires the presence of each and every member of a certain group of employees. Right before starting time, your assistant hurries in to inform you, "Melissa just called to say she's running late and won't be here for another half hour." You could have guessed it would be Melissa; it would never be your most exceptional employee, Jessica. The only way Jessica would be late is if she saw a terrible car wreck on the road and stopped to administer CPR to an infant. And even then, she would arrange a conference call from her cell phone while racing to the office so she wouldn't miss anything.

As a leader, it's your job to check for monkeys in every situation, even the smallest interactions.

Where's the monkey? It's on *your* back, because the meeting can't take place without Melissa, and the tasks you hoped to accomplish will have to be tackled another time. There are also monkeys sitting on the backs of all the good employees who came to the meeting. Their work has been delayed, thanks to the slacker; they'll have to accommodate the rescheduled meeting. They also each have what I call an Anger Monkey sitting on their backs: they're angry at Melissa for being late, and they're angry at you for allowing Melissa to throw off everyone's work.

Now suppose Melissa showed up on time, but she sat in the back of the meeting room with a couple of loser friends, making "amusing" comments while other people were speaking, showing each other funny videos on their iPads, and so on. Naturally, Melissa and her buddies would miss all the important information brought up at the meeting, and only half pay attention to the instructions they're given.

Now who's got the monkey? Every other person at the meeting. Because Melissa and friends interfered with the smooth running of the meeting, the others have more work to do—*and* more resentment toward Melissa, her friends, and the boss who seems unable to corral the miscreants.

Bad employees don't care if their monkeys are running wild; they're not upset to see work pile up or the department falling behind. They're not distressed that other employees or the manager are forced to take on their work—heck, they're happy! In fact, the less work they have to do, the happier they are. Don't look for the monkey on the back of the bad employee, because you won't find it there!

> Bad employees don't care if their monkeys are running wild; they're not upset to see work pile up or the department falling behind. In fact, the less work they have to do, the happier they are.

Let's say you're a bank manager concerned about customer relations. Eager to gather information, you instruct the tellers and other staff members to fill out an interaction report for each customer, every day, five days a week, for the next six months.

Where is the monkey? On the backs of the good employees who have to waste their time filling out the reports and are now worried. ("If he wants me to fill out a report, I must have been doing something wrong," these good folks tell themselves.) The monkey is certainly not on the backs of the bad employees, because they care little about delivering good customer service and even less about filling in the reports (which they probably won't do properly).

What if you head up a department that requires every single employee to punch in and punch out at the time clock: Is there a good reason for this requirement? Did you institute this rule because two out of a hundred employees weren't on time? If so, you've put a Resentment Monkey on just about all of your employees, and stuck an Extra-Work Monkey on the back of someone who now has to keep track of the time records.

This is admittedly a fine line to walk. Sometimes you can't avoid putting monkeys where they don't really belong. There may be a good reason for the time clock, but if you're aware that everything you do has the potential for creating monkeys, you can try to limit it. Would it be possible for you to require *only* the offending employees to clock in? So what if those poor performers are upset: at least you haven't "monkeyed with" the good employees.

Ask for Help

It's not always obvious where the monkeys are, so it pays to ask. You don't need an elaborate program; just talk to people. I was at the bank recently when a woman walked up to me and said, "Hi, I'm Fran, the manager of this branch. How are things going?"

"Fine," I replied. Then a thought struck me. "Actually," I said, "I do get annoyed at that teller over there who always does crossword puzzles. He never makes eye contact."

It's not always obvious where the monkeys are, so it pays to ask. You don't need an elaborate program; just talk to people.

Fran thanked me for the information, and you know what? I never saw that teller doing crossword puzzles again. You might think it would be obvious that the teller wasn't doing a good job and that a manager who walked by him many times a day would have noticed he was shifting monkeys to customers. However, Fran wasn't aware of everyone's point of view, so she missed the problem.

As a manager, you may shy away from asking your customers how things are going because you don't want to risk taking on more monkeys. It's much easier to do nothing and wait for the problem to explode. Handling problems while they are still small, however, will lower the future monkey population. And if you don't ask your customers for feedback, you might be leaving them stuck with the monkey, which is exactly what you don't want. Remember, it's not your customer's job to deal with a lazy teller—that's your responsibility. It's *your* job to know where the monkeys are, and asking will help you find them.

Handling problems while they are still small will lower the future monkey population.

You can also ask your good employees about out-of-place monkeys. Remember the monkeys shifted by the boss who had every clerk push the premium membership program? Something like that can easily shift monkeys to customers, too. With new initiatives like this, it's helpful to check in with your best clerks—and *only* your best clerks—to ask if pushing the membership is worth the effort. They deal with the customers every day; they know exactly how it's going over. You might get answers like, "Well, I did sign up three people yesterday, but five others, including Mrs. Smith who shops here all the time, told me they didn't like feeling so pressured." If five people actually told the clerk they were unhappy, you can bet another forty or fifty were also upset but didn't say anything.

Flush Out Hidden Monkeys

Monkeys are not always immediately obvious, which is why you need to look for them every time you walk into a room, join a meeting, enter a conversation, or interact with people in any way—or even when you think about your people and organization.

When you walk into the work area at your place of business, ask yourself if everyone is doing the tasks he or she is supposed to. Are some of the slothful employees pushing their work onto others? Are some of the really good ones doing things you haven't assigned to them?

When you walk into a meeting, ask yourself who is most comfortable and who is least comfortable. Are two or three negative people sitting together, probably in the back of the room, right by the door, or otherwise far away from the leader? If so, they're in a comfortable position that encourages them to goof off or, at the very least, be inattentive.

Consider the following questions as well:

- Is your organization as a whole treating the customers and clients well, or behaving as if they were untrustworthy or guilty?

- Does management help all workers understand how they are coming across to others?

- Do the least-effective employees shoulder at least part of their own monkeys?

- Do the managers issue rules that make the good people resentful?

- Are your top performers forced to follow procedures that may be helpful for the so-so ones, but get in the way of the best people?

The supply of monkeys is unlimited, and we can find them anywhere and everywhere, whether we're at work, at home, or at play. Being aware of who has the monkey in any given situation and figuring out who *should* have it is critical to the maintenance of a balanced life. None of us can avoid having some monkeys on our backs, but let's make sure they are rightfully ours and that we don't have an entire troop of them!

Learning to recognize the out-of-place monkeys and then shift them back to their rightful owners is one of the most important lessons you'll ever learn. This doesn't mean avoiding responsibility; it means putting responsibility where it belongs, which will make you a much better leader, parent, friend, and person.

Now that we know how to identify the out-of-place monkeys, it's time to look in depth at the three principles for shifting them back where they belong, which chapters 4, 5, and 6 will address:

1. Treat everyone well.
2. Make decisions based on your best people.
3. Protect your good people first.

In the next chapter, let's start with treating everyone well.

Always remember:

✽ As a leader, it's your job to be on the lookout for out-of-place monkeys.

✽ Ask for help from your customers and best employees to find those monkeys.

* Don't just look for out-of-place monkeys on the backs of your employees; check your customers' backs as well.

Chapter 4

Treat Everyone Well

1. Treat everyone well.
2. Make decisions based on your best people.
3. Protect your good people first.

Treat everyone well. Doesn't that sound like a strange idea? Why should liars, criers, and slackers be treated well? Shouldn't they be scolded and forced to toe the line? While it may be tempting to scold, the truth of the matter is scolding doesn't work.

Up until now we've been talking about life in the business world, but as I've said before, monkeys shift in all areas of life. The principles for dealing with them—especially the first principle, treat everyone well—apply universally.

My wife and I love to go shopping for antiques, and we find ourselves in a lot of antique stores where we see signs that say something like:

> Pretty to look at,
> Nice to hold,
> But if it gets broken,
> **CONSIDER IT SOLD!!!!**

Now, my wife is completely driven by guilt. If she thought she had damaged something, she would run up to the store owner, apologize, pay for it, and then rush home to bake the owner a casserole as a token of apology. She's very careful about handling things in antique stores and has never broken anything yet. When she sees a stern warning sign, however, she starts to worry about spending too much time in the store. She fears that the longer she's in the store, the greater the chance she'll break something. Owners who post signs like this don't realize that many people are like my wife: they could become valuable customers, but instead they are much more likely to leave the store quickly because the sign makes them uncomfortable.

Why would an owner put up a sign like that? Perhaps there was a time when someone broke something valuable, put it back on the shelf, and crept away without paying. Unfortunately, posting a sign won't stop careless or criminal people from handling the merchandise. It just upsets careful, honest people. And the more threatening the language on the sign, the more likely those honest people will hide a broken item simply because they are afraid of facing a wrathful, unreasonable owner. Because one person did something wrong, the sign was put up to clamp down on everyone. The net result? Good customers like my wife hesitate to stay in the shop.

Of course, it's not just antique stores: all kinds of stores have signs proclaiming "Shoplifters Will Be Prosecuted!" and "We Are Watching You!" These signs create Worry and Guilt Monkeys, but those monkeys aren't on the backs of the careless or criminal customers. They already know what they're doing is wrong; that's why they hide it. Trying to limit the harm by putting a monkey on everyone's back can backfire and destroy the positive relationships and customer loyalty that store owners really want.

And in the workplace, punishing everyone for the misdeeds of a few takes the monkeys off the backs of the bad employees and puts them squarely on the backs of the good employees. That's why the first principle of shifting the monkey is to treat everyone well—good customers, bad customers, potential shoplifters, employees, obnoxious drivers—*everyone*.

> The first principle of shifting the monkey is to treat everyone well—good customers, bad customers, potential shoplifters, employees, obnoxious drivers—*everyone*.

Rise to the Challenge

Treating everyone as if he or she were good is one of the biggest challenges we face in life. We must do so for a very simple reason: our actions validate the good, responsible, productive people and make the irresponsible, lazy, unpleasant people feel uncomfortable. This is a key concept because, unlike you and me, irresponsible people don't feel uncomfortable when they're treated poorly. They're used to it; they expect it. It doesn't shift the monkey to their backs. But when you treat them as if they were good, it's a whole different story.

Unfortunately, it's all too common to treat people as if they were all jerks. Teachers often do this: for example, because one student stole a box of pencils from the supply cabinet and won't admit it, the entire class must write an essay on the importance of being honest. The dishonest student recognizes himself in the punishment, but thinks everyone else is like him and that it's OK to be substandard. The responsible, honest students, on the other hand, are angry, frustrated, and discouraged. Where's the monkey? On the backs of the very best people.

> Treating everyone well validates the good, responsible, productive people and makes the irresponsible, lazy, unpleasant people feel uncomfortable.

In order to be effective leaders, we need to change this approach and act as if everyone is a good person. This can be difficult, largely because we're used to being treated poorly, but treating all people as if they were good can do much to keep the monkeys in their proper place.

1. Where is the monkey?
2. Where should the monkey be?
3. How do I shift the monkey to its proper place?

I first thought about treating everyone as if they were good when I was a student. One day, when class was in session and all the students were in their classrooms, two of the biggest troublemakers in school walked down the hallway past our door. The teacher stuck her head out into the hallway and yelled, "You two had better get to class! Do you have a pass?" She automatically assumed they were up to something bad and treated them accordingly.

A few minutes later, the student body president and head cheerleader walked down the same hallway. This time, the teacher smiled and waved as they walked by. No yelling. No demands for passes. She automatically treated them as if they were good.

While the two troublemakers probably *were* up to no good, and the other two students almost certainly had permission to be out of class, the teacher treated both according to their reputations rather than their present actions. What other option did she have? She could have ignored the students in the hall, but that would have been a weak response; it was her job as a teacher to nip potential problems in the bud. A better solution would have been to politely ask *every* student in the hall, "Hi, can I help you?" The students' replies and body language would have made it plain if they were out to make trouble or do legitimate errands, and the teacher wouldn't have offended anyone.

The same applies in customer service. We want to keep shoplifting to a minimum, yet we don't want to insult our customers. How can we achieve both goals? Approach all customers as if they were responsible, law-abiding citizens, and never avoid them. It's as simple as a clerk politely saying, "Hi. May I help you?" The good customer feels appreciated by the warm greeting and offer of help regardless of whether she needs it.

Amazingly, this also accomplishes both of our goals: every customer is treated with respect, *and* the threat of shoplifting is reduced because the occasional bad customer now knows the clerk is watching. The good, responsible customers become more loyal, while the negative ones become uncomfortable. The monkey is exactly where it's supposed to be.

How does the principle of treating everyone well work in the office arena? Remember Melissa, the slacker employee who called right before the big meeting to tell you she wouldn't be there?

The obvious response to this kind of behavior is to get angry and frustrated. You might try the tough-love approach by sending a blanket email that establishes a new draconian policy regarding punctuality. Of course, the overwhelming majority of employees are not late, and the bad ones will continue their irresponsible behavior regardless of the new policy. So now the monkey is on the backs of the good employees while the bad ones get away scot-free. This strains the work atmosphere, increases employee resentment and dissatisfaction, and doesn't solve the problem. The "act as if everyone is guilty" approach simply doesn't work.

> Approach all customers as if they were responsible, law-abiding citizens, and never avoid them.

Where is the monkey in this situation? On the backs of the manager and the good employees. Where should it be? On the backs of the Melissas. Who is responsible for shifting the monkey back where it belongs? You, the leader.

When employees don't follow through with required tasks, or they blatantly break the rules, you need to take the issue directly to those few who behave inappropriately—not with ineffectual criticism, but with firm enforcement of your expectations. Handling the problem correctly will shift the monkey back to them, increase their level of concern, and prevent them from handing off monkeys to others. Let's look at some typical situations and ways to respond.

Ignore Excuses

Suppose you had asked a less-than-reliable employee named John to prepare a report, and the deadline is today. You could treat him as if you expect him to be irresponsible by asking, "Have you had a chance to finish that report?" Odds are, he hasn't and will bury you under an avalanche of excuses.

Instead, you could inquire, "How did that report turn out?" You've assumed John is a good employee and finished the report on time. Now the monkey sits squarely on John's back. If, by some miracle, he has completed the report, he can feel good about himself. If he hasn't completed it, it's up to him to decide whether to lie or tell the truth. The monkey stays where it belongs.

But suppose John instantly begins reeling off excuses: "Well, I couldn't finish because I haven't been feeling well, and then I had to go on a bunch of service calls. I really tried, but doing those service calls just sucked up all my time!"

Don't engage in conversations about excuses. Don't question the excuses, don't sympathize, and don't argue. Just keep asking how the report turned out.

If an employee makes an excuse and the leader responds to it in any way, it becomes the employee's go-to excuse. When the Johns of the world tell you their children were sick, the copy machines were broken, the person they had to speak to didn't respond to their calls, or whatever, don't let them sidetrack you. Become a broken record.

Don't engage in conversations about excuses. Don't question the excuses, don't sympathize, and don't argue.

If John replies, "But I told you I haven't been feeling well," you say, "I need that report at three o'clock today."

When John tries again with "I had to do all those service calls," you respond, without any anger or sarcasm in your voice, "I need the finished report at three o'clock today."

Where is the monkey? On John's back, where it belongs.

Poor performers like John cannot provide structure for themselves, so you must provide it by saying, "I need the report on my desk, at three o'clock today, complete and stapled together." Make your instructions very clear so that both you and the poor performer know the difference between right and wrong. When the issues are clear and John still doesn't perform, there's no Guilt Monkey on your back as you discipline him.

Sidle Up

Sidling up literally means "approaching from the side." Instead of storming right up to a bad employee and getting in his face, try appearing at his side. Negative people, especially those with strong personalities, can't stand it. They love to draw a line in the sand. They thrive in an oppositional environment, standing on their side of the imaginary line, glaring across at you with arms folded. That is why you never want a desk, countertop, or anything else between you and a negative person. The barrier actually empowers that person!

> Negative people thrive in an oppositional environment, standing on their side of the imaginary line, glaring across at you with arms folded. That is why you never want a desk, countertop, or anything else between you and a negative person.

Think of it this way. If an angry person barges into your office, who takes on the monkey? You do, because you are not prepared for this confrontation. The angry person is less likely to have a monkey on his back, especially if setting up angry confrontations is his typical modus operandi; that is, if he uses anger as a weapon and expects people to respond to it.

But suppose you take away the anger. As long as you keep the desk between yourself and him, he is in his preferred environment, and you are uncomfortable: the monkey is on your back. If you remain on the opposite side of the desk, you never will be able to shift any part of your monkey to him. If you move to the other side of the desk, however, standing side by side as if you were best friends, you'll find you have an opportunity to share that monkey with him.

Stop Blaming Everyone for the Behavior of a Few

Treating everyone well is a key principle in shifting the monkey. By extension, this also means not treating everyone poorly. Never address an entire group regarding the negative behaviors of a few. Don't let a few bad apples drive how you treat everyone.

> Never address an entire group regarding the negative behaviors of a few.

This mistake often occurs during big meetings, or through mass emails or corporate memos, and sounds something like this: "Some of you have not turned in your reports yet. The deadline was an hour ago, and we need them now!"

The good news is that a blanket scolding will shift the monkey. The bad news is that it shifts the monkey off bad employees and directly onto your most valuable employees. As soon as the high achievers hear the announcement or read the email, they'll run down to the manager's secretary and ask, "Did you get my report? I made five back-up copies and have one at home in the refrigerator just in case the house burns down!" They have Concern Monkeys on their backs, and a monkey has popped up on the back of the secretary as well—a Reassurance Monkey. This explosion of new misplaced monkeys is the exact opposite of what you hoped would happen.

Another unwanted result is that the underachievers —the people for whom the announcement, email, or memo was intended—are actually relieved. Because the entire group was admonished, the underachievers think, "Oh, good. There must be a whole bunch of us who haven't finished the report, so I don't look so bad!" Addressing the entire group actually took the monkey *off* of their backs.

As a leader, you must have the courage to approach your ineffective employees on a one-to-one basis. This kind of interaction is much more powerful than general announcements or blanket emails. You might simply approach the employee—sidle up if need be—and ask in a professional, nonsarcastic manner if he had any problems with the report he turned in that morning. (Ask this question even if you know he didn't turn it in.) This puts the monkey back on the employee. It may be tempting to use a cutting tone, but that's not productive; it creates conflict, and bad employees thrive on conflict.

> You must have the courage to approach your ineffective employees on a one-to-one basis.

So while it's easy, and sometimes tempting, to spray the whole group with a certain message ("Some of you have been late for work!" "Some of you need to dress more professionally!" "Some of you are not providing excellent customer service!"), you need to be sure that you don't make the problem worse. Shift the monkeys back where they belong, and don't create new ones for people who are already meeting expectations.

Stop Avoiding Irresponsible Employees

We often make things easy for irresponsible employees by giving them less to do. And on those rare occasions when we do give them a task, we hesitate to follow up on their progress. We just don't want to hear their excuses and find ourselves in the position of having to counsel or discipline them. Better to let sleeping dogs lie, we think.

The situation goes something like this: let's say you're managing a store, and a customer calls to complain about how one of the clerks treated her. You ask the clerk to call the customer and apologize, and even give him specific phrases to use so that he can handle the task effectively. The next day you dread following up, because you assume the clerk did not call the customer to apologize. You feel a burden as you trudge toward the clerk and hesitantly ask, "Did you get a chance to call that customer?"

By approaching him in this way, you're already letting him off the hook. He can now say, "Oh, I tried but the line was busy," or "I just didn't have time because we were swamped yesterday." Now you have to ask him again to make the call and follow up a second time.

1. Where is the monkey?
2. Where should the monkey be?
3. How do I shift the monkey to its proper place?

Instead, try this: approach the clerk confidently, as if you are certain he met your expectations, and ask, "What did the customer say when you called and apologized?"

Do you see the difference in the two approaches? Instead of balancing the monkey on your own back, you have shifted it back to the clerk, simply by treating him as if he were a good employee. If he actually did follow up and complete the task, he has an opportunity to share the experience and feel good about himself. If he did not call the customer, he can admit he didn't do what you asked—which is very uncomfortable—or he can flat-out lie, saying something like, "I called and left a message, but she never called me back."

Treat Lies as Truth

What should you do if you're fairly sure an employee is lying to you? You might be tempted to tell him so, but don't. Instead, treat him as if he was telling the truth and respond in an affirmative way. In this example, you might say, "Thank you so much. I'll call her now to see how she reacted to your message. Can you give me the number you called? I want to touch base right away as a follow up." If the clerk was not honest, believe me, he will feel the monkey.

Whether the clerk will behave more responsibly in the future is an open question, but I can tell you he will have learned one lesson: do not lie. Meanwhile, you will have gained credibility as a leader and validated all of the honest and hard-working employees while putting additional pressure on *all* of the irresponsible employees. The monkey ends up perched exactly where it belongs.

Issue Big Threat Monkeys Only With Great Caution

1. Treat everyone well.
2. Make decisions based on your best people.
3. Protect your good people first.

You can extend the concept of treating everyone well by refraining from adding an "or else" when providing structure and instructions, as in "Turn the report in on time, or else you will be docked two hours' pay!" Once you lay out the consequences, the slacker knows exactly what will happen if he fails to perform. He can decide whether it's worth it, and there's a very good chance he'll conclude it's OK not to complete the report: "Only lose two hours' pay? I can live with that." Don't bother trying to put a Punishment Monkey on a bad employee's back, because known consequences are easier for him to handle. And you don't need to put Punishment Monkeys on the backs of your good employees, of course, because they already want to do the right thing.

> Don't bother trying to put a Punishment Monkey on a bad employee's back, because known consequences are easier to deal with than the unknown.

Threats don't work, especially threats you know you can't carry out. Sooner or later someone will call your bluff, and then everyone will know you've been trying to manage them with Ghost Monkeys. Once they see at least one Ghost Monkey, they'll begin to think that all of your threats are empty. This loss of credibility will hurt you with the good employees as well as the bad. In addition, when you don't follow through on threats, you diminish the power of those consequences in the future and your ability to shift monkeys back where they belong.

If you do pull out your Big Threat Monkeys, as in "Turn the report in at three o'clock, or you're fired," you had better mean it. If you back off, you'll look like a fool, a weakling, or both. Correcting the mistake later on won't help. Suppose, for example, you've threatened to fire Sue ten times, but don't. Then on the eleventh time, you actually do fire her. Finally firing her doesn't enhance your credibility; it weakens it. Even the good employees, who used to think you were all bark and no bite, will become afraid of you. They'll take on Uncertainty Monkeys: they see you've changed the rules of the game, and now they'll question everything you say and do.

Big threats are dangerous; don't use them unless you have to. This doesn't mean you are unprotected; the mere fact that you are the leader gives you power in the form of *Implied* Threat Monkeys. Simply issuing instructions, clearly and firmly, without getting caught up in excuses or complaints, places Implied Threat Monkeys on their backs.

> Big threats are dangerous; don't use them unless you have to. The mere fact that you are the leader gives you power.

Harness Peer Pressure

Emotional Monkeys are also quietly effective. You use them when you say things like, "I noticed in our meeting that a few people rolled their eyes after your comments. I'm just telling you because I'd want to know. . . ." or "I sure hope others didn't misinterpret what you meant when you said . . ." By framing the point in terms of what you would want to know, you've made an inarguable statement. You're also treating the employee as if he were a good employee who has a conscience and would want to know if he offended others. In fact, he probably knows he's not a good employee, and he's afraid others know it, too. You're letting him know his secret's out, and not just with you. Good employees will respond to *your* approval or disapproval, but the slackers are more likely to respond to *peer* approval and disapproval.

Not all bad employees will respond to an Emotional Monkey, but issuing one that doesn't work won't hurt your credibility or diminish your power because it's based on peer pressure. It also allows you to treat the bad employee as if he were good: after all, you're telling him, with great concern, how he looks in the eyes of his peers.

If, and only if, the Implied Threat and Emotional Monkeys fail should you move up to your Big Threat Monkeys by issuing threats to dock pay, give a bad performance review, and so on. If you do, be sure to give very clear performance instructions—and follow through on each and every threat.

Control the Desire for Revenge

We all have the impulse to take vengeance, but effective leaders never use Revenge Monkeys. They will never, for example, berate a bad employee publicly just to see him squirm. Effective leaders don't want their bad people mad; they want them good, or they want them gone.

Think about what happens when the leader takes revenge on the screw-up employee. Instead of "seeing the light" and miraculously becoming a model employee, she'll probably harass her peers and snap at the customers. There's a very good chance that she has her own very large Revenge Monkey—more like a Revenge Gorilla—that she'll unleash by deliberately scaring off customers, driving a good employee to quit, or even sabotaging a deal your company is working on.

Sort Out Ignorance From Insubordination

Suppose Natalie missed the Monday morning staff meeting. Since she's a new employee, it's not clear why she failed to be there. Did she not know about the meeting? Did she know, but not care? Or is she a really good worker who has an excellent reason for not being there?

One of the key challenges in dealing with employees who do not perform properly is sorting out whether they are ignorant or insubordinate. If they are ignorant—if they don't understand their duties or have difficulty performing them—some coaching or training may solve the problem. If they're insubordinate and don't care about their duties, however, no amount of teaching or coaching will help.

> A key challenge in dealing with employees who do not perform properly is sorting out whether they are ignorant or insubordinate.

Because you have no track record with Natalie, and you want to treat her as if she were good, you could approach her privately and say, "Natalie, is everything OK?" Notice that there's no accusation, no threat, not even a mention of the missed meeting. There's no hint of negativity at all, just a question backed by genuine concern.

If Natalie responds by apologizing for missing the meeting, you know she's most likely a good employee who knows the difference between right and wrong. If, on the other hand, she responds with a blank stare, you have to sort out whether she didn't know she was supposed to be at the meeting or just didn't feel like going to the meeting. You can do so by mentioning that she wasn't at the meeting—again, with concern rather than anger: "You weren't at the meeting this morning. Is everything all right?" Natalie's response should tell you all you need to know. If she's embarrassed, she probably didn't know about the meeting or didn't realize she was supposed to be there, so you can educate her. If she starts in with a barrage of excuses, you know you'll have to watch out for monkeys.

Sometimes people blame their performance on so-called external reasons: "I wanted to be there, but I was waiting for the carpet guy to install my new carpet, and he said he would be there last week, but he wasn't, and if I didn't get the carpet by Tuesday, there wouldn't be another chance until next Friday." Others use excuses they think sound reasonable, like "No one told me about the meeting." But of course it shouldn't be your duty (or anyone else's) to issue reminders about every meeting.

Don't let anyone use excuses to shift the monkey—or to demonstrate to others how easy it is to shift the monkey under your supervision. Make a mental note of what the employee says, and if she uses that excuse or a variation of it again, you know it's her go-to excuse. In that case you must become the broken record, laying out the structure very clearly: "The Monday morning staff meeting starts promptly at nine o'clock in conference room three."

Since Natalie is new, you might add, "Walk with me, and I'll show you where the room is." If she's late next Monday, you'll know she's insubordinate.

In short, analyze the problem by determining first whether the problem-maker is insubordinate or ignorant, and second whether the problem is a one-time or recurring event. Begin by approaching the employee with concern, not anger or accusation, as this shifts the monkey back to the employee; now she must decide whether to lie, confess, explain, or try to wiggle out of it. There's always the chance she has an excellent reason for missing the meeting; she may say, "I was meeting with the company president" or produce a note from the doctor proving her child was indeed ill.

Deflect "The People's Representative" Attack Monkeys

One way ineffectual people dole out monkeys is by pretending that they are representing a lot of other folks. They'll approach the leader and say something to the effect of "You know, a whole bunch of people are unhappy with the decision you made," "A lot of people are upset with the way you handled this" or "You really upset a lot of people at the last meeting."

Bad employees often try to rattle the leader with this kind of Attack Monkey. Your best response, as always, is to treat them well. Suppose your best employee told you that something you said or did hurt a lot of feelings. You would believe she's telling the truth, so you would instantly respond by saying something like, "Thank you so much for telling me. I'm just sick about this. I owe a personal apology to you and to everyone whose feelings were hurt. If you get me a list of those people, I will personally apologize to every one of them."

This response would demonstrate your concern for your people and your desire to make things right. You would lift the burden of a Concern Monkey from your good employee and simultaneously increase your credibility as a leader.

Now suppose your worst employee approached you with the same message. You're sure there's a 99 percent chance he's making it up. So how should you respond? Treat him exactly the same way, with the same response: "Thank you so much for telling me. I'm just sick about this. I owe a personal apology to you and to everyone whose feelings were hurt. If you get me a list of those people, I will personally apologize to every one of them."

By treating the worst employee as if he were the best, you shift the responsibility to him. He has to come up with a list of offended employees, which is most likely impossible because you probably didn't offend anyone. In addition, he's now got a Responsibility Monkey on his back, and he doesn't want it. "I can't get you a list," he might stammer. "Those people wouldn't feel comfortable with you coming to them; they just wanted me to represent them."

> By treating the worst employee as if he were the best, you shift the responsibility to him.

You would then ignore his protests and say, "Just get me the list, please. I'd really like to apologize." Every time he tries to wriggle out with another excuse, politely ask for the list. You're teaching him not to lie to you, because you'll call him on his lies.

When you see him the next day, however, don't bring up the list. Why? Because he's ready for you. He'll have a new set of excuses. That's good, because it means he's uncomfortable around you because he has been dishonest. Besides, if you keep bringing up the list day after day, he'll soon see that there are no consequences for not giving you the list, and your Fear Monkey will become weak. Instead, wait for him to come to you with some other negative complaint or attempt to shift a monkey. Then ask him about that list. This trains him not to bring up phony complaints or instigate negative situations. He'll learn that every time he brings you a problem, you'll remind him of his monkey.

Follow the Golden Rule

Are we treating people well? Employees, family, friends, clerks, strangers, and everyone else? Just because we have been treated less than exceptionally doesn't mean we need to perpetuate offensive practices that only create more monkeys.

Recently, my son and I were checking out at a chain bookstore. The clerk asked me if I was a "Loyalty Reward Card" customer. I replied that I did not know, but there was a pretty good chance my wife was. The clerk gave me a suspicious glance and said she would need to confirm it first. She asked for my name, which she entered into her computer. Her next inquiry was my home address and phone number. But there was more. She then asked my work email address and cell phone number to confirm it was really me. I guess I passed the test because she didn't call another clerk over, shine a bright light in my eyes, and perform the good cop/bad cop routine. Instead, she sighed and said, "I guess it's you." When I gave her my credit card to pay for my books, she announced in a disgusted tone, "I'll need to see your ID." The only response I could think of was to inquire how that loyalty program was working.

As I was standing there with the clerk, I thought, "Who has the monkey? I have it. Why should the customer trying to purchase something have the monkey? Something is wrong here."

Now, you might say the clerk was just doing her job, that the real problem was a company more worried about sneaky customers trying to "steal" reward points than the majority of customers who are the key to their success. But she *personally* made the choice to treat me poorly, which leads me to my point: it's essential for each of us to reflect on what we're doing, how we're leading our organizations, and how we're living our lives.

> It's essential for each of us to reflect on what we're doing, how we're leading our organizations, and how we're living our lives.

Change the World One Person at a Time

Here's a good example of how treating everyone well can change the world, if only in a small way.

Years ago I visited a new church. When I walked in, I saw some rows of empty pews in a prime location, with only one person, an elderly matron, sitting in that area. I walked over there, smiled, and sat down near the lady. As soon as I had taken my seat, I sensed the lady was not happy about it. She seemed to be scowling at me! Assuming it was just my imagination, I smiled at her and turned my attention to the front of the church.

A minute or so later, the cutest couple I'd ever seen, an old man and his wife in their mid-eighties, walked down the aisle, looking around as if it was their first visit to the church, too. They were adorable—the husband's necktie matched his wife's dress. After a minute or so spent mulling over the seating options, they sat on the other side of the church lady. I could instantly tell that she didn't like that, either, as she turned and stared at them coldly. I hoped they didn't notice. After all, we were in church!

When we all got up to sing the first hymn, the old man was unsure which song we were singing, so he leaned over and whispered to his wife, "What hymn is it?" His wife whispered the hymn number. The church lady then snapped her head toward them, put her finger to her lips, and hissed out a mean, "Shhhhh!"

Guess who never went back to that church again?

In this situation, who had the monkey? This nice couple. Who *did not* have a monkey? The mean lady. Something was wrong here. Over the next few Sundays, I noticed that if a couple with young children sat within three rows of the church lady, she stared daggers at them until they became so uncomfortable and nervous about their children's behavior that they retreated to less desirable seats.

After a month or so of observing reactions like this, I realized that the entire church was afraid of her.

I heard people say things like, "I hope she thought the hymns were appropriate," and "Do you think she thought the sermon was OK?" Apparently, the church lady had trained the entire church to accommodate her every whim—and to read her mind to *anticipate* her every whim.

Everyone was afraid of her ... except me. I thought the whole thing was ridiculous. All of these nice people had monkeys on their backs; everyone, that is, except the church lady. That needed to change. So, I decided to shift the monkey.

When the church lady walked into church the following week and everyone scattered, I sought her out. As soon as she came into view, I half-sprinted over to her, put my arm around her shoulder, and greeted her with, "That is the cutest little sweater you have on! How are you doing today?" It wasn't long before she started avoiding me like the plague. She started sitting in the back corner of the church, where, for a change, *she* accommodated the *other people* who sat there. Over time, by treating this mean person as if she were polite and kind, the members of the church shifted the monkey back where it belonged. And they finally got their church back.

There is a great example of what can occur when you treat a negative person with a positive attitude. When you offer a warm greeting and a compliment, positive people will like it, and perhaps even seek you out next time. The negative people? They'll be uncomfortable, and forced to change their own behaviors.

Always remember:

* Threatening your customers with dire consequences, just because a few crummy ones
  harmed you in the past, puts a monkey on the
  back of every customer.

* The best approach is to treat your customers,
  employees, and everyone else as if they are
  good, responsible, and honest. This validates
  the positive, hard-working people and makes
  liars, criers, and slackers uncomfortable.

* Treating bad folks as if they were good helps
  shift monkeys back where they belong.

* Be careful not to treat an entire group poorly
  just because a few people are rotten apples.

* Sidling up is a key technique for dealing with
  negative folks, especially those with forceful
  personalities.

* As a leader, you have your own monkeys at
  hand, but you must use them with caution.

Chapter 5

Make Decisions Based on Your Best People

1. Treat everyone well.
2. Make decisions based on your best people.
3. Protect your good people first.

Sometimes people confuse shifting the monkey with "killing them with kindness." These are actually two very different approaches. When you kill them with kindness, you direct all of your efforts toward the negative people. You try to be so nice that they'll see your point of view and change their behavior, or you shift some of the load off their backs until they can see what it's like to get caught up (which never happens), or something similar. Unfortunately, lavishing too much positive attention on the ineffectual folks can be very disheartening to the majority of people, the productive ones.

Consider your current management approach. If a few people are working too slowly, do you put a keystroke counter on everyone's computer? Install a punch clock because a few come in late? Make everyone fill out lengthy forms documenting this or that because a few slackers are not touching all the bases?

If you do, you're putting a Worry Monkey on the backs of your best employees, who will fret about being fired if they're one-half of one-percent less than perfect. You're also proving to your bad employees that they're right to see you as a miserable jerk, enticing them to think up new ways to circumvent the expectations, and provoking them to get back at you by making phony complaints to HR. You know exactly who is not pulling his or her weight. Why hand out Guilt and Resentment Monkeys to your entire staff?

You know exactly who is not pulling his or her weight. Why hand out Guilt and Resentment Monkeys to your entire staff?

In contrast, when you shift the monkey, you focus on the exceptional people. That's why you should always make decisions with your best people in mind, rather than your worst. Emphasize the good people, not the bad.

Thank the Good Folks

Many years ago, I was a high school principal faced with all the usual problems, including a small group of teachers who seemed to major in dodging responsibility. One of the duties they dodged most enthusiastically was standing in the packed hallways during passing periods when the kids were walking from one class to another. They always had excuses for staying in their rooms at these times—and the excuses sounded so similar I began to suspect they were all using the same list.

We needed teachers to supervise during passing period because kids will be kids, and that means something unpleasant is bound to happen in the hallway. Often, it's a scuffle. Most principals become frustrated when this happens and at the next staff meeting will angrily say, "There were two fights in the hallway last week, and no teachers around to handle them! I've told you repeatedly that you need to stand in the hallway during passing periods, and it's clearly written in the handbook. Don't you people pay attention? Don't you care? From now on, *all* of you will be in the hallway during every passing period, or there will be consequences!"

1. Where is the monkey?
2. Where should the monkey be?
3. How do I shift the monkey to its proper place?

The problem with this approach is that it focuses on the bad people and suggests that everybody is potentially bad. It also emphasizes bad behavior. The really good teachers who diligently stand in the hallway day after day will worry they didn't get out there soon enough or stay long enough, and the pretty good teachers who only failed to show up once or twice will be consumed with guilt. The monkey is on the backs of the really good and pretty good teachers. The bad teachers, however, don't have any monkeys because they don't care one whit. In fact, they'll feel safe because the principal yelled at *everyone*, which to them means they're no worse than anyone else and can continue ignoring their duties. The principal's efforts, then, will fail because they are based on the actions of the worst teachers.

How about a different approach? What would happen if you thanked the good folks for their good work? I once stood before the teachers at a meeting and said, "I really want to thank those of you who have made that extra effort to be out in the hallway between classes. Today I saw two boys who were about to fight in a hallway where a teacher was present. I don't think the teacher even saw them, but right before they got into it, one of them looked up, saw the teacher, nudged the other student, and pointed to the teacher. Then they walked their separate ways. The teacher prevented a fight just by being there. So thank you for being out there. It makes our school a better place for our students and for the rest of us."

Telling people when they're doing a good job shifts the focus away from bad employees and the bad things that have happened in the past. It spotlights the good employees, models good behavior, and gets the group in general to think about how they can prevent future problems. In my example, the teachers who diligently stood in the hallways felt validated, and each one thought I was talking about him or her!

This group-praise approach is better than singling out one teacher, who might become the target of jealous, negative attention as a result. By thanking the entire group, I publicly reinforced the desired action, rather than an individual person. Later, I privately thanked the teacher whose presence stopped the fight. This technique worked, and I'm happy to report that many more teachers began to stand in the hallways during passing period. Some of the negative people probably started going out into the hallways just to see who belonged to the goody-two-shoes group. They were out in the hallway for the wrong reason, but you know what? I didn't care. As long as they were in the hallway, I was happy.

Telling people when they're doing a good job spotlights the good employees, models good behavior, and gets the group in general to think about how they can prevent future problems.

Thanking the good folks isn't just a good idea in the workplace; it is important in service groups, churches, and every other kind of organization. It can be especially helpful in non-work settings where people serve as volunteers and are not concerned with career advancement, salary, or similar workplace factors.

If you're in a leadership position at your place of worship, for example, you can stand up and say something to the effect of "I'd like to thank everyone who volunteered to rake the leaves, tidy up the lobby, and do so many other things to make our building beautiful. I was so proud to see so many of you helping out."

Thanking them in this way—publicly, as a group— makes it seem as if the group of helpers is large and contributes to the sense that everyone helps and goodness is rewarded. As a leader, you want each slacker who did not help out to think that everyone else volunteered: *you're all alone, you're not included.* Some of those folks who did not pitch in will feel like they missed out on something special.

You might think this is a case of preaching to the choir; after all, these helpful people would have shown up anyway, without being thanked. Well, I say you *should* preach to the choir, because otherwise they might stop showing up. You can go even further by individually thanking them, either in person or with a nice note.

Give Anonymous Public Praise

This technique we've been discussing is not only public and group oriented, it's anonymous. This allows the leader to include a large number of people in the praise, focus on good behavior, and encourage the bad folks to improve their behavior, even if only for a while. There are several ways to use anonymous public praise, beginning with your daily or weekly communications.

Suppose all of your employees are salaried, so there's no additional pay for putting in extra hours. Despite this, some of your best people have been coming in and working extra on the weekends to make sure they finish up the report, get fully prepared for the big client presentation, and so on. At the next company meeting you can address the entire group and say, "I want to sincerely thank those who have been coming in on the weekends—it has made such a difference! We've picked up additional clients thanks to the extra work you've done on your own time. I am so proud to be affiliated with people who are willing to work that hard!"

Using anonymous public praise makes the good people feel rewarded for their efforts; protects them from being mocked by the slackers; creates a sense that lots of people are pitching in, so if you're not, you're missing something; and allows you to privately praise the good folks later.

Use Borrowed Praise

You can take the technique even further by using "borrowed" praise. For example, a lot of companies send regular emails to all employees reminding them of certain things, identifying the "Worker of the Week," introducing new policies, and so on. You can add a little article that anonymously and publicly praises an employee's good behavior: "Thanks so much to all of you who work so hard to make our store great. Just the other day, I saw a customer talking to one of our employees, and as the customer walked away she said to her daughter, 'That's why I like to shop here—they're so nice and helpful!' You really create customer loyalty. Keep up the good work!"

Notice that you don't praise the employee yourself; instead, you expand your circle of influence by quoting a real customer. You seem to be talking about the past, but your message is really about the future, when all employees will conduct themselves in pleasant and helpful ways every single day.

Feed the Desire for Recognition and Autonomy

Thanking your good people for desirable behavior and giving anonymous, sometimes borrowed public praise are two management techniques that will put the emphasis on your best people. You can take that a step further by thinking ahead about your best employees when making a decision or formulating a policy.

1. Treat everyone well.
2. Make decisions based on your best people.
3. Protect your good people first.

Most of all, your best people want recognition and autonomy.

Recognition means acknowledging that what they're doing is different, better, and beyond what others do. For years I was blessed with an assistant who was head and shoulders above the others. Do you know how she knew that she was my best employee? I told her so, over and over again. By the way, recognition doesn't mean handing out "employee of the month" plaques, as this usually becomes a rotating honor that sooner or later lands on almost everyone's desk. Even when the plaque is really given out to the best, it can harm morale. Imagine that you have ten or fifteen very good workers, one superstar, and several slackers. Naturally, the superstar will always win employee of the month, which means that every single month the group of very good workers will feel like they just got a kick in the rear. "What's the point of trying," they'll tell themselves and each other. "We're never going to win."

Recognition can be a raise or promotion, but you can't always offer that. Fortunately, a private conversation is a powerful way of recognition. You can privately tell your great people, "You are the best employee in this organization. I recognize that and appreciate everything you do for us." You can also recognize the very good people by telling them, privately, "I want you to know that you are a key player in this organization," or "You are unbelievably good. I don't know what we would do without you." You're not lying when you say these things, because you're not saying they are the very best. They might interpret it that way, but you're being truthful when you say they are critical and you don't know what you'd do without them.

Autonomy means that when people are doing something well, you don't slap on a bunch of cumbersome requirements to make sure they do it the "right" way or the same way everyone else does. Why should your top salesperson have to follow the standard sales script when pitching a client? The top people have the gift of sales; they don't need to follow scripts written for so-so salespeople who lack the gift and genuinely need help. In fact, the top salespeople should be *writing* the script! It's true that 80 percent of salespeople need the script, and so we try to be fair by making everyone give the same pitch. I say give the good people the autonomy to make their own decisions. Instead of giving them a Discouragement Monkey by forcing them to follow the script, let them follow the instincts that make them great sellers.

> When people are doing something well, don't slap on a bunch of cumbersome requirements to make sure they do it the "right" way or the same way everyone else does.

With top performers, feed their desire for autonomy. Ask their opinion when you're preparing a new policy or procedure. Instead of hiring an outside firm to prepare a new sales script based on the latest theories and focus group results, talk to your best salespeople. Ask them what works for them and what they would like to see in the script. If you've commissioned an outside firm to prepare the script, show it to your best producers before giving it to everyone; ask them what they think about it, what works, and what doesn't. Not only will you get very valuable input from these people who know exactly what it takes to make a sale, but you'll also be recognizing their contribution to the company.

You can't ask your best people for their input on everything—sometimes new rules or procedures come from the higher-ups or are legally mandated, and sometimes getting more input just isn't practical—but whenever possible, get their input. It's much better to have policies geared toward encouraging super-star behavior than to have policies that limit every employee.

Learn to Ignore

A key part of basing your actions on your best rather than your worst people is learning to ignore the bad ones. I don't mean you should be rude or pretend they're not there, but you can turn a deaf ear to them when they start trying to shift the monkey.

Suppose Joe, the manager, is making his morning tour of the department—greeting his staff and checking on the status of various projects. When he comes to Sue's desk, he gives his usual greeting: "Good morning, Sue! How are you doing?"

Sue, who is one of the worst employees in the department, launches into her usual round of complaints. "Oh, you wouldn't believe how far behind I am. Frank didn't get me the info I needed until 4:57 yesterday afternoon! And these new project requirements? I don't know how I'm going to work them in, what with the budget and time restrictions. *And* my mother-in-law is sick. And you know what else? My allergies are acting up!"

Many managers would sigh and say, "All right, I'll have Anna help you. Give me one of those files; I'll take care of it myself." Now Sue's monkey has reproduced! She's shifted two, one for Anna and one for Joe. For Sue, the day is shaping up quite nicely, and it's only 9:00 am.

How do you deal with situations like this? Ignore them. When Sue finishes her litany of complaints, simply say, "OK, have a nice day," and move on to talk with the next employee. Don't sympathize with Sue, don't argue with her, don't roll your eyes and mutter under your breath. Don't do anything but wish her a good day and move on. Remember, *anything* you do to engage Sue starts the monkey-shifting process. If you sympathize, you'll wind up reassigning or taking on some of her work. If you argue, you'll be hit with an avalanche of grievances and complaints, and you'll both wind up angry (which just proves to Sue that you're out to get her). If you roll your eyes and mutter under your breath, you can be sure she'll notice and take that as proof she is not appreciated and should try even less in the future. Holding back and just saying "Have a nice day" may seem hard, but managing difficult people requires that you first manage yourself.

This doesn't mean you should ignore everybody. If a good employee tells you something is wrong or that she isn't up to the task, you should respond appropriately because you know she's not trying to shift her monkey. She genuinely needs your input or assistance. Neither would you ignore a new employee; you don't yet know if his complaint is genuine, so you treat him as if he were an excellent employee. But when you know the complaints aren't valid—when you run into a Sue—treat the complainer like a good, competent person who can take care of those non-problems without you—by walking away.

As you develop your ability to ignore, your bad employees will complain less, because they'll learn that complaining simply doesn't work anymore. You won't give in or engage with their demands in any way—not with scolding, not with negotiation—just as you wouldn't give in to a spoiled child throwing a tantrum in order to get candy.

As you develop your ability to ignore, your bad employees will complain less, because they'll learn that complaining simply doesn't work anymore.

Nobody repeats a behavior indefinitely without a reward, even if that reward is negative attention (like getting into an argument). Much of the time, problem people do get a reward—often from a supervisor or another authority figure. They wield their poor behavior as a weapon to gain power, intimidate others, and lighten their loads. Knowing this, when an employee, customer, volunteer, or neighbor displays negative behavior, ask yourself: Is he using his negativity as a weapon? Does he seem to use that weapon repeatedly? If so, he's being rewarded for using it; for rolling his eyes, crying, sighing, getting angry, yelling, using sarcasm, staying tight-lipped but giving a cold stare, and so on. These are often the go-to weapons of problem people, and if you respond, they'll keep using them. If you ignore them, however, they'll eventually realize their best weapons are ineffective.

They'll have to try some other approach; hopefully one that's more positive.

> Nobody repeats a behavior indefinitely without a reward, even if that reward is negative attention.

When you have to deal with these people, always remember that they're used to angry, head-on confrontations; quiet approaches from the side make them uncomfortable. If you see them start to turn toward you, you know the sidle-up is working. Greet them, give them instructions if that's what you're there for, and ignore all their attempts to use negativity to shift the monkey.

Focus on Actions Rather Than Thoughts

During my speaking engagements, I often talk about using anonymous public praise, learning to ignore, and other management techniques based on the best people, instead of the worst. At some point, an audience member inevitably raises his hand and says, "But you're not changing anyone's mind with these techniques."

I always reply, "You're absolutely right. And you know what? I'm not focusing on changing their minds. I care about improving the behavior."

You don't have to worry about changing the thoughts of the good people. They've already got the right ideas and attitudes and will only need gentle reminders and assistance. They'll do a good job because they want to; they're driven by the desire to be excellent, please customers, get a raise, and achieve goals. You just have to help them learn and grow, pat them on the back when they do a good job (which is most of the time), and help them discover what went wrong when things don't work too well (which is rare). Similarly, good customers will not shoplift, abuse your return policy, or pass bad checks. You don't have to "make" them behave with harsh warnings and policies.

As for the bad folks, you *can't* change their thoughts. Putting up nasty signs, devising harsh contracts, creative punitive work rules, and hiring armed guards won't make them think or act like good people. In fact, these things may just make them work harder at being lazy, bad, or just plain crooked. Where bad people are concerned, the only thing you can change is their behavior.

> Where bad people are concerned, the only thing you can change is their behavior.

It's important to understand that while you, the leader, might believe people should do something because they care about the company, your only real concern is that they do it. Yes, everyone should greet the customers and treat them with courtesy because that's the right thing to do, but it's more important that they perform the action properly than believe in treating people well. It doesn't matter if they do it because they're hoping to get promoted, because they feel peer pressure, or even because they're afraid of being fired if they don't. All you care about is that they do it properly.

If they eventually come to understand the importance of the action and embrace it as their own, so much the better. Some will get it. For example, if you're heading up the complaint department for a department store, you might tell all of your customer representatives to let the complaining customers tell their entire story before interrupting, and then to say, "I'm sorry you had a bad experience with us." The bad customer representatives may not want to listen and may not really be sorry, but when they start listening and apologizing, they'll find they have better interactions with customers. As a result, some employees will embrace the required technique. They may do so for the selfish purpose of making their own lives easier, but that's fine, because they're doing what they're supposed to be doing.

> Some employees will embrace required techniques for the selfish purpose of making their own lives easier, but that's fine, because they're doing what they're supposed to be doing.

Your workers don't need to like their jobs; they just need to act as if they do. They don't have to like the customers, just simply act as if they do. Here's a little technique that can help people "act as if they do" even when they don't: begin saying something out loud, and finish it in your head. If, for example, you have to apologize to a customer, you can say, out loud, "I'm really sorry we didn't live up to your expectations," and then add, in your head, "because your expectations were unreasonable." You can say "I'm really sorry we didn't live up to your expectations" with genuine sincerity, because if things had worked out you wouldn't have to be dealing with this complaining customer.

Reward Effort, Not Just Results

As your bad and so-so employees begin to improve, start thinking about rewarding them—not for their tremendous accomplishments, but for their effort. The truth is, you're often better off rewarding effort rather than results. That may seem odd; after all, isn't it the results that count? They do count, quite a bit, but often the effort is what really matters.

Imagine you're running a sales department with one superstar who handles the best territory, a bunch of fairly good salespeople, and a few slackers. You certainly want to reward effort, and probably do because commissions are tied to employees' sales: more sales equals more money. But how about effort? Suppose Amy, one of your so-so salespeople, starts going out on twenty cold calls a month, instead of the usual ten. If I were her boss, I would definitely let her know how much I appreciate that effort, even if only one of the additional calls led to a sale.

Or think about a basketball team that plays well but loses in the last second thanks to a fluke shot by the other team. If you only reward results, you'll berate the team, which certainly won't encourage them to play hard next time. But if you reward their effort, you'll have the opportunity to encourage them to play even harder in the next game.

Remember, luck can play a role in success. Some people are naturally more gifted, or they may have a better territory to work in. If you only reward them because they perform well, you'll discourage the many others who are trying hard and want to do well.

Get the Most Out of Bad Employees

Refusing to let bad employees shift the monkey is a big first step—but then what? If they're uneducated rather than insubordinate, you can help them improve their skills. But what if they're lazy, uncooperative, or otherwise just no good?

In an ideal situation, you could fire them and never have to deal with them again. That's not always possible, though, or it may take a long time. You could try encouraging them to transfer to other departments if you work in a large company, but there's a good chance the other department managers have heard about the problem employees and won't want them either. Sooner or later, you're going to get stuck dealing with less-than-desirable employees. It pays to know how to get the most out of them without spending a great deal of your time and energy supervising their every move.

It pays to know how to get the most out of difficult employees without spending a great deal of time and energy supervising their every move.

One way of dealing with a problem employee is to have him do something routine and relatively unimportant, like stocking shelves or filing. When he whines about the job, don't sympathize with him, help him, or get someone else to help him. In fact, don't interact with him at all, other than to give very clear instructions. Be very clear about what you expect, saying something like, "Here's your work; here are your guidelines. Report back in one hour." The menial work must be real work that needs to be done, and you must make clear that however dull or mechanical the task, you expect it *will* be done. Good employees may be aware these ineffective people are doing different or less work, but they'll be glad the slackers are actually doing *something* for a change. And they'll be relieved not to be doing those menial tasks themselves!

Where is the monkey? Squarely on the bad employee's back. He might decide to do the job properly, in which case you can thank him. There's a small possibility that this will be the first time he's been praised for a job well done. If he likes it, he may start to improve his overall performance. But odds are, he'll goof off and not complete this simple task. That's OK, because you'll have an obvious example of poor performance to document, and you'll be one step closer to getting rid of him.

Another way to deal with a bad employee is to give her a task that is not important to the overall performance of the group or company, like a holiday party. Some years ago I was in charge of about 100 people, most of whom were hard-working and dedicated to their jobs. Naturally, a small number of people specialized in dodging responsibility, verbally bullying others, disrupting departmental meetings by drifting in late and making irrelevant comments, and dashing out early on the flimsiest of pretexts. I quickly realized that these people were, in effect, running the department by keeping everyone else off balance.

Determined to turn this around, I decided to go on the offensive. At a staff meeting, I brought up the holiday party months before it was usually discussed. Instead of asking for volunteers to plan it, I appointed the three biggest problem employees to the party planning committee. "This is going to be the best party we've ever had," I said enthusiastically, in front of everyone. "We're eager to hear your ideas and want you to report on your progress at every meeting from now on."

I didn't really expect these three to plan a great party, but I now had some leverage. Every time they tried to shift the monkey with their usual litany of complaints, I would ask them how the party planning was coming along. "We're all counting on you to throw the best party ever," I'd remind them. "What are your plans?"

When these three behaved normally, I did not bring up the party planning, but when they tried to shift the monkey to me, I added to their woes. I would begin each department meeting by asking the same thing. This directed everyone's attention to them and forced them to stammer out their excuses for not having made any progress.

For the rest of the year, I had those employees on the run. Any time they acted up—and often before they even got started—I asked about the party plans. I never criticized them, put forth my own ideas, or offered to help. I just kept asking about the fabulous party they were planning for their friends and coworkers. Every time I did, they would slink away with their tails between their legs.

In this kind of situation, whether the party or other project is a success is almost irrelevant. Public responsibility puts on huge pressure. If the party is a success, you can make those people out to be heroes. If the party bombs, now everyone in the company sees the problem—and it frees you up as the supervisor to take the steps necessary to get the slackers out of the company.

Base Decisions on the Best Customers, Too

This principle applies to customers as well as employees. In what ways are you potentially driving away business by basing your decisions on your worst customers? For example, do you make every customer who wants to return something jump through hoops, even though you know that 99 percent are legitimate returns? Will preventing a small number of bad returns make up for the business you'll lose when word spreads about your super-tough return policy? Let's look at some examples of decision making based on the worst people or situations.

Not too long ago, I went into a gourmet market in an upscale neighborhood and was surprised to see an armed guard standing just inside the front door with a grim look on his face and a pistol in his gun belt. Perhaps management was trying to make the customers feel secure by hiring armed guards, but my reaction was, "Whoa! This market must be a dangerous place if they need a guy with a gun standing by the front door!"

Curious, I asked the manager if there had been a rash of muggings at the store, or if gang members were intimidating the customers. "No," he said.

"There were some problems in a store in a different state, so headquarters decided every store would have an armed guard."

1. Where is the monkey?
2. Where should the monkey be?
3. How do I shift the monkey to its proper place?

This is a case of higher management making a decision based on its worst-case scenario. Because there were security problems in one "bad" store, *all* stores must have armed guards. This decision places a big fat Fear Monkey on the back of every customer and employee in all of its stores. Customers may hurry through their shopping because they're worried something bad will happen; they may even decide to shop elsewhere. Employees may find the work atmosphere oppressive and start to wonder if they are in danger. Why hand out *any* Fear Monkeys in the good stores? Why allow the bad stores to harm the profits of the good?

Everybody—management, employees, and customers—wants an appropriate level of security, and that may include armed guards in the really dangerous stores. Wouldn't it be wiser, though, for management to keep the armed guards out of the relatively safe stores? Or at least disguise them? Perhaps they could use plainclothes guards, security cameras, or a combination.

Shifting the monkey to all customers indiscriminately is a problem in all types of businesses. I was talking to a professional speaker who proudly told me that his contract was "as thick as a brick." He smiled and explained,

"I've got protective clauses for everything! Any way a client might try to screw me, I'm protected."

I asked, "Have you ever had a problem with a client?"

"Just a few," he answered. "Nothing serious. But I never will again."

"If you've only had a few minor problems, how did you know which protective clauses to include?"

"Well," he said, "I talked to other speakers. One told me about a problem he once had, and another told me about a problem he once had, and so on. I gathered them all together and *voila*! A super-protective contract. Nobody will ever give me any trouble again!"

In other words, this guy didn't even wait for trouble to hit—he reacted ahead of time, creating an iron-clad contract with so many restrictive clauses it undoubtedly scared away plenty of potential clients. I give many speeches every year and know from firsthand experience that thick, super-restrictive contracts can be counterproductive. This speaker was making decisions about his contract based on the worst possible clients—clients who weren't even his!

I approach the same situation by acting as if all my clients are the best possible people, keeping my contract very short. It's possible that a client will cheat me—it hasn't happened yet, although you never know—but I would rather not begin our relationship by putting a Tough Contract Monkey on everyone's back. A super-restrictive contract or policy may protect you in the worst-case scenario, but will that compensate for the bad feelings you create in every scenario, and the potential business you scare away?

Similarly, when I give public speeches, I never begin by asking the audience to turn off their cell phones. I never mention cell phones at all, in fact. That's because I know someone's cell phone is going to ring anyway, and if I've made a big deal out of it, all the attention would be diverted to that ringing phone. That would put a monkey on my back (do I respond or ignore it?) and on the backs of the audience members as they wait to see what I do.

A super-restrictive contract or policy may protect you in the worst-case scenario, but will that compensate for the bad feelings you create in every scenario, and the potential business you scare away?

Apply These Techniques to Customers, Too

Many of the strategies discussed in this chapter can also be used with troublesome customers. Take ignoring, for example. If you manage a restaurant, for example, you're bound to get a certain amount of complaints from your customers about the quality of the food, the prices, and the customer service. Suppose a customer who has been eating in your restaurant for a couple of years tells you a certain waitperson did not provide good service. Naturally, you would apologize, thank him for having brought the problem to your attention, and perhaps offer him a free meal next time he comes in.

You would certainly not ignore a good customer like this. Neither should you ignore a complaint from a brand-new customer. Since you don't know what type of customer she might turn out to be, you would act as if she is an excellent customer.

But then there's the customer who complains over and over again about nothing and is clearly a problem. It might be a certain customer who comes in regularly, and every third time complains that the food is spoiled and refuses to pay her bill. After you've seen this happen a few times, you know that you're being had. The next time she complains, you say, with regret, "You know, you haven't enjoyed our food for several visits. I'm concerned that we won't ever be able to please you. I hate to see you waste your money, so I want you to know we won't be able to offer any more refunds." You've treated her as a good customer, whose happiness you value, and you've solved your problem. You may lose her as a customer, but that's OK. She's the type who relishes the drama of the complaint, and she will waste as much of your time as you'll allow. You can't allow that; you must ignore her.

An idealistic young friend of mine in his twenties leads volunteer groups every summer to India to participate in leadership training for working with orphans and other underprivileged children. He's found that in every group of volunteers at least one person complains about everything—the weather, the food, the transportation, the noise, the accommodations, the tasks he's asked to do, and so on. This person always has something negative to say and insists that the situation is unfair or, at the very least, not right. My friend has tried placating these complainers, rearranging things to suit them, being sympathetic, and jollying them out of their bad moods, all to no avail. Now he doesn't even try; he simply turns a deaf ear. If they insist that he listen, he will tell them they have two minutes to lay out their complaints, then he has something important to do. He will listen, nod, and then say, with a smile, "Yeah, that's the way things go, isn't it?" Then he turns and goes about his business. They don't completely stop complaining, he tells me, but they do it less because it doesn't get them anywhere.

Remember Who's in the Majority

As leaders at work and elsewhere, we're all blessed with a few problematic people. Don't worry; if you miss a chance to deal with one today, you'll get another chance tomorrow. They've been plaguing organizations for a long time. But here's something that's easy to forget: *most people are not bad.* As a leader, you may be tempted to treat everyone as ineffective, perhaps because you've been hurt by bad people in the past, or because you're trying to prevent trouble before it starts. However, taking that approach never works well, as you know if you've ever been in an airport security with an irritable guard barking instructions at everyone because one person forgot to take her shoes off.

So remember that most people are good and should be treated accordingly. So far, no one has figured out how to turn bad people good, but you can prevent them from shifting the monkey and can contain their damage by keeping your focus on the good people.

Always remember:

* Think about what your best workers and customers would want.

* Make sure the outstanding people know they're outstanding. Don't treat everyone the same, as that's very discouraging to high achievers.

* You're not expected to fix the bad people, but you are expected to control them.

* If you don't make the difference between right and wrong very clear, your best people start to lose confidence. They will ask why they're trying so hard, when other people get away with doing substandard work but are never reprimanded.

* Give your good workers the gift of confidence by showing them you are a strong leader who will protect them from crummy peers and reward their efforts.

Chapter 6

Protect Your Good People First

1. Treat everyone well.
2. Make decisions based on your best people.
3. Protect your good people first.

Suppose you're running the regular monthly meeting when Claude stands up, cuts you off, and says, "I just want you to know that I'm really unhappy about . . ."

He does this all the time: interrupts the meeting to talk about his personal complaints, even though they're not on the agenda. He's had plenty of opportunities to bring the issues up with you before, yet he's wasting the time of all the good people who need to accomplish things during the meeting.

For negative people such as Claude, dominating meetings is a standard technique. Unfortunately, you might accept the monkey by talking about the problem, as many leaders do: "OK, Claude, this isn't on the agenda, but let's take some time to talk about your concern." All the good people roll their eyes. They know the meeting has been shot, and you're not protecting them (or yourself) against Claude. On the other hand, you might be tempted to respond with sarcasm instead, or even to berate Claude for wasting everyone's time—but that would upset the good employees who don't want to see you behaving in any way other than with a dignified manner.

To protect your good people first in this situation, you could instead say to Claude, "That sounds like something I need to know more about. I'll be happy to come in early before work and review this with you. In fact, I'd love to. You name the day."

By doing this, you decline to accept the Time-Wasting Monkey from Claude, and shift the Responsibility Monkey to him. There's an excellent chance Claude *won't* show up for an early meeting, because while problem employees are often willing to waste the leader's and their peers' time, they can't stand to invest a minute of their personal time on work—especially for a nonsensical complaint. You protect your good employees by guarding their time and preventing Claude from giving away monkeys. At the same time, you get a chance to sort things out: if Claude actually does come in before work to talk to you, his problem may be important and worth the time.

Give Good Employees Permission *Not* to Volunteer

Protecting your good people first is very important; they make your organization work. Always remember that your good people carry a much greater monkey load than others because they try so hard to be great. It's your job as a leader to lighten their load whenever possible and to make sure they don't take on any new monkeys that are not important or necessary. In short, you'll need to protect them not only from the bad employees but also from *themselves*.

Good people are so driven by responsibility and the desire to make sure the company runs well that they tend to be the first to volunteer for extra duties and to handle a problem when they see it arise without being told to do so.

The good news is, the company does well because these employees take on extra work. The bad news is, these same employees can eventually wear down and stop taking up the slack. In the meantime, the bad employees' miserable behavior is validated because it has been tolerated. They've learned that it's OK to be slackers. And the employees that fall somewhere in between great and lousy learn they don't need to try harder, because there are no punishments for slacking off and no real benefits for going that extra mile.

When great employees take on all the extra work, others learn they don't need to try harder, because there are no punishments for slacking off and no real benefits for going that extra mile.

As the leader, you must protect your good employees by making sure that only the most important monkeys are on their backs: not the extra monkeys that others have more room to carry, and certainly not other people's monkeys. They should only carry the really difficult monkeys that you believe only they can handle.

One way to do this is to give your great people permission *not* to volunteer. Think about what typically happens when a leader issues a blanket call for help. Let's say Allison, a department manager, needs someone to head the new Emergency Preparedness Committee. At a staff meeting, she asks for volunteers and notices that almost everyone looks down, turns their heads away, inspects their fingernails, or finds other ways to avoid making eye contact. The tension in the room builds until Eric, one of the few great employees, can't take it anymore. He raises his hand and says, "I'll do it."

The other employees are relieved to know that they won't be stuck with that chore, and Eric feels good because he's helping out and knows the task will be done properly. But Allison should feel pretty bad, because her best employee is now saddled with another monkey that any half-decent employee could have easily handled. It's a waste of Eric's time and talent, both of which should be spent on more crucial assignments. The slacker employees have successfully dodged responsibility once again.

Allison needs to prevent situations like this by giving Eric permission not to volunteer. She can do this by speaking to Eric ahead of time, saying something like, "Eric, I'm going to be asking for a volunteer to head up the Emergency Preparedness Committee. I know you're always the first to volunteer, and I really appreciate that, but unless this is your dream assignment, let somebody else volunteer. I give you permission not to do anything."

If it's not possible to speak to Eric ahead of time, Allison could wait until he volunteers and counter it with something like, "Thanks for volunteering, Eric, but I've got something else for you to do. Who else can take this on?"

Giving Eric permission not to volunteer prevents a Guilt Monkey from jumping on his back; he carries enough of those already as he strives to make everything turn out perfectly.

Let Them Know What's *Not* Their Job

A lot of managers avoid confronting certain ineffectual employees and their bad behavior, hoping other employees or customers will somehow fix them. They may hope, for example, that enough glares and nasty comments from customers will cure bank teller Betsy's bad behavior, or that peer pressure will get Jason, who rips his colleagues with sarcasm, to cut it out.

It's your job to put a stop to that. For example, if you have three night custodians, and one of them typically spends part of the night sleeping, it's not up to the others to wake him up and try to get him to work—or to do his job for him. They should simply continue to do their jobs as diligently as possible. If certain things don't get done, that's the bad employee's problem, and by extension, the manager's problem.

Help your employees create reasonable boundaries. This is not to say people will never help anybody out or do anything that isn't clearly spelled out in their job descriptions, but the division of responsibility should be clear to all so that good employees don't end up shouldering others' responsibilities. You can expect your good employees to know what is right, but you can't expect them to fix bad coworkers or bad work, just as you wouldn't expect your children to fix their misbehaving friends.

As a leader, make it clear to your good employees that slacker employees are *your* responsibility, not theirs. I tell my workers, "When somebody does something wrong, or just doesn't do what he's supposed to do, it's not up to you to fix it. That's my job. I need you to keep on doing the great work you're doing. Keep on doing what's right even when someone else is doing what's wrong."

> Help your employees create reasonable boundaries. As a leader, make it clear to good employees that slacker employees are *your* responsibility, not theirs.

You may want to say privately to a good worker, "Frank, I want you to know I really appreciate the great work you do. I know your coworkers aren't as productive as you are, but that's their problem, not yours." Or you may publicly acknowledge the entire custodial crew because the building is in such pristine condition: the floors gleam, the windows sparkle, and visitors constantly comment on the spotless lobby. Then, later, you can privately say to Frank, "I know you're the one carrying the weight, and I really appreciate it." Frank will appreciate the fact that you are aware of his exemplary performance.

People build up "monkey tolerance" when they know someone is looking out for them—they don't mind doing a little more because they know the leader is aware of their great efforts and will back them up. This helps them withstand the monkeys they naturally put on their own backs because they are high achievers.

Take Away Burdensome Responsibilities

You naturally delegate important responsibilities to key personnel because you know they'll do it right. Often, however, that means they now have to deal with the jerks, and that can drag them down.

Suppose, for example, certain members of your sales team travel frequently, and you've assigned one of your top assistants, Leah, to handle all travel arrangements. It's crucial that this task be handled properly, as the salespeople must respond to existing clients and land new ones. The good salespeople always give Leah proper notice about their travel schedules and work with her to make sure everything goes smoothly. Larry, however, frequently fails to give Leah the information she needs until the last minute and rarely tells her about any changes, so his plans are usually a mess. He often misses flights or doesn't have a rental car when he arrives at his destination. He complains long and loud about this, letting everyone know what he thinks about Leah's "failures." This puts a monkey on Leah's back, even though she wants nothing more than to do a good job but can't, because of Larry.

Larry has abused the privilege of using Leah's services, so the best thing to do is take them away. From now on, insist that Larry book his own flights and make all the other arrangements. This instantly removes the monkey from Leah's back and puts it on Larry's: if he misses a flight or the rental car isn't available, it's his fault. You might be afraid to make the switch, correctly figuring that Larry will miss a lot of appointments. That's probably true, but he was already missing a lot of appointments—and handing out monkeys to boot!

> 1. Where is the monkey?
> 2. Where should the monkey be?
> 3. How do I shift the monkey to its proper place?

Bad employees are always getting into fixes; there's no reason to let them drag others down with them. Take the responsibility for their problems away from good people, and put the monkey back where it belongs: on the back of those who should care the most about solving the problem. This also lets you assess their performance and then discipline or teach them accordingly. Meanwhile, your good employees are very happy because you've protected them.

Ignore Minor Errors

As leader, you should ignore slackers' attempts to shift the monkey. You must also ignore the minor errors of high performers. In practice this means that when a slacker makes an error, you point it out. By doing so, you're treating him like a good person who wants to take responsibility and to improve. You add to his responsibility load, which you know is pretty light in reality. But your best people already feel responsible; they carry a huge responsibility and guilt load. You don't need to add to it, and you shouldn't.

It's inevitable that even the best people will occasionally do something wrong, but the high achievers already carry around a 600-pound Guilt Gorilla. When they make errors, they know it. They feel sick about it and go over and over the error in their minds. Don't upbraid them for their errors, or even bring the errors up—at least not directly.

When an error occurs, ask yourself: does Sally know that she made a mistake? If the answer is yes, there's no need to bring it up. If Sally doesn't know, you should bring it up in the mildest possible way. For example, let's say you're the manager of an accounting department, and she got some figures wrong in a report. Approach her in a friendly way and say, "Sally, I wonder if I can get your help with something. I was looking at this report and was a little confused by . . ." Then you can go through the report with her and "discover" the error together. Once you know that she is aware of the mistake, you can be confident she will correct it and never make that mistake again.

Another way to communicate with great workers about errors without adding to their monkey burden is by putting blame on yourself. Suppose you've never told your new assistant how you'd like the telephone to be answered, and she's been doing it differently than you'd like for several weeks. If you just tell her what to say, she'll immediately comply because she wants to do a great job, but she may now have a Guilt Monkey on her back for having done it "wrong" in the past. So try saying something like, "Nena, I'm a little picky in that I have this certain way I like the phone answered. I wrote it down here on this card. Would you mind hanging on to it so you can show it to any temporary worker who might fill in for you sometime?"

Instead of correcting her, or even acknowledging her error, you've asked her to do you a favor. You can be sure an excellent worker like Nena will memorize the card in no time flat and will answer the phone exactly the way you want from now on—with no monkeys added to her burden.

Delegate to the Right Person for the Job

We live in an egalitarian society, and many leaders pride themselves on saying they wouldn't ask their people to do anything they wouldn't do themselves. Well, I totally disagree with that philosophy. As a leader, I'm always asking people to do things I wouldn't even think of doing, because that's better for the organization. For example, I would never climb on the roof to see if the shingles are loose because, for one thing, I'm terrified of heights. Conversely, the maintenance guy isn't afraid of being out on the roof, and he's an expert at making repairs, but he's terrified at the thought of dealing with angry clients who need to be placated. I don't mind dealing with the angry customers. Our unspoken deal—the building custodian takes care of the roof, and I take care of the customers—makes perfect sense and creates a more profitable company.

Delegating is a major key to success. When used well, it ensures employees are doing what they are best at. Never do something someone else can do, because there are certain things only the leader can do, and that's where you must focus your attention. This is just like keeping your best people from volunteering for menial tasks, because there are certain responsibilities that only they can handle. Remember, you are one of your best people.

> Delegating is a major key to success. Never do something someone else can do, because there are certain things only the leader can do, and that's where you must focus your attention.

When thinking about who should receive which assignment, I remind myself that my best employee can do everything well, but I need to keep him free to attend to the most crucial tasks. For example, I work at a big university that, like all universities, is very eager to receive large donations from corporations and wealthy people. For years, our athletic foundation was headed up by a very talented person who could do everything and did so willingly, even handing out programs at sports events, licking envelopes, and filing alongside the lowest-level employees. He was a great guy, but he should have been spending all of his time raising money and going after that billion-dollar gift, not doing low-level chores. Every minute he spent licking envelopes was a minute he was *not* bringing in donations that the university depended on.

Treat Everyone Well, but not Equally

Your people are *not* equal; they excel in different areas and should be treated accordingly. It's OK to give preferential treatment to your superstars, as long as you also give everyone else an opportunity to improve and shine.

If you're running a sales department, and you have a star salesman, feed him by giving him the big leads. If you hand the leads out equally to all of your salespeople, some of your best possibilities will be put in the hands of your worst producers, and your numbers will go down. When someone like Bill Gates calls to discuss a purchase, I certainly don't want him transferred to Alice Average or Doug Do-Nothing. I want him to talk to Samantha Superstar. Is that unfair? Not at all. It's your responsibility as leader to make sure the organization thrives.

> People excel in different areas and should be treated accordingly.

It's the same in any business; the big producers deserve extra attention and support. It's your job as leader to identify and support the big producers—and at the same time, offer advice, training, or other aid to all of the less-skilled people who are striving to become better producers. Of course, feeding your best producers doesn't mean you deliberately starve your lesser producers. You wouldn't give every good lead to your star salesperson, while handing the worthless leads to everyone else. This would exhaust your best employees and demoralize your lesser employees.

If, for example, I managed a sales department and had to divide the territory into five parts, one for each salesperson, I wouldn't give 90 percent of the territory to my two superstars and let the other three fight over the remaining 10 percent. That would be foolish. Instead, I would give everyone territories of roughly equal size, but draw the lines in such a way that my most important clients are in the territories of my two best performers. That way, my best clients and best salespeople are protected, but my lesser salespeople also have a chance to be successful while learning and growing.

It's your job to identify and support the big producers—and at the same time, offer advice, training, or other aid to all of the less-skilled people who are striving to become better producers.

Similarly, if I were running a real estate office, I would not use a simple rotation system to determine who gets the phone-in or walk-in clients (such as, first client to salesperson 1, second client to salesperson 2, and so on). Instead, I would have the receptionist give the clients a brief list of questions to answer that would help us determine which potential client goes to which salesperson. I would also make sure all the salespeople knew about this system so the good producers would be aware that I know who they are. They would understand that I am giving them the best clients because I know they are great workers, and I have faith in them. They would appreciate that and, as a result, work hard for me.

Let me be clear: the high performers would have worked hard even without this system, because that's the kind of people they are. But they would have been expending energy on a lot of the smaller clients, which is not the best use of their time and is not as profitable for the company.

Unequal treatment should be the rule in every aspect of leadership, including decisions about whom to fire during the lean times. Suppose you oversee five different departments, and you're instructed to cut your overall budget by 10 percent. A weak manager will simply make equal cuts to the budgets of all five departments and lay off the same percentage of people from each. He would assume that doing so is fair and will protect him from criticism. A strong manager will make the cuts with a surgical scalpel, deciding which departments and employees are vital and which are not. This would open him up to all kinds of criticism, but he will have retained the good people on whom the company really depends. There's a chance in a poor economy that you might have to lose some good people; that's no fun. However, make sure it's not your best people, and always ensure your weakest employees are first to go.

> Unequal treatment should be the rule in every aspect of leadership, including decisions about whom to fire during the lean times. A strong manager will make the cuts with a surgical scalpel, deciding which departments and employees are vital and which are not.

Shield Good People From Envy and Resentment

More often than not, your stellar employees will be envied and criticized by others who feel they are teacher's pets. As a leader, you'll need to stand up and protect your good people, which means that if some employees are resentful, they should resent *you,* not your good employees.

One year when I coached basketball, I had just one standout player, Justin. I was planning to use Justin heavily but didn't want the other players to resent him. He already had the burden of having to carry the entire team; he certainly didn't need the added trouble of envious and sullen teammates.

As it happens, Justin was a modest guy who never hogged the spotlight and was happy to let his teammates take their share of shots. He just wanted to fit in and have some fun. But that wouldn't help the team succeed, so I gathered the guys together and told them we were only going to win if Justin scored big every game. "If Justin is open," I told them, "pass the ball to him. And if Justin misses three shots in a row, give him the ball again anyway." Looking at Justin, I said, "Your job is to receive the ball from your teammates and shoot. If you do not shoot, I will take you out of the game."

Now the game plan was perfectly clear, and if anyone was mad about it, they were mad at me, not Justin. I gave him permission to be a ball hog and deflected all potential criticism toward me. My job was to make sure the team had a winning season, not to win a popularity contest. (By the way, we had a winning season.)

Protecting your good people does more than allow them to perform well; it also helps them be a positive influence on others. Most of your good, well-rounded people work hard to be respected by their peers, which gives them an opportunity to "speak" on the leader's behalf and to defend him and the organization. For example, if the workers are unhappy about a new policy, the good person might say something like, "Let's wait to see how this shakes out," or "Let's give it a try and see if we can't make it work."

> Protecting your good people helps them be a
> positive influence on others and to defend the leader
> and the organization.

Your good people are naturally on your side, so they can bring the others along. But if their peers stop respecting them, they lose the ability to teach, lead, and sway others toward the leader's viewpoint. It's in your best interest as leader to protect your best workers so they can keep doing that.

Take the "Hit" for Good People

Another way to ease your good employees' monkey burden is by letting them know you'll stick your neck out for them. You can demonstrate this dramatically by shouldering the responsibility on occasion when they make mistakes.

Suppose you have a terrific assistant named Alex who botched an order. He ordered the wrong merchandise, and there's a chance you'll be stuck with it or at least have to pay extra to get things straightened out. An average leader might say to poor Alex, who already feels terrible, "Well, now we're in a lot of trouble!" or "What are you going to do to fix this?" Perhaps he'll call the company that sent the merchandise and say, loud enough for Alex and eight other people to hear, "My assistant really goofed up the order, so I'm calling to see what we can do about it."

A great leader, however, would take a different approach by calling the company to say, "Unfortunately,

I messed up this order, and now I'm wondering if I can get your help in straightening it out."

By taking the hit for Alex, you've made a friend for life. Doing so for all your good people will cause them to work even harder for you, because they know you're on their side. You lose nothing, because it's ultimately your responsibility to straighten out the mess, and you gain everything by validating your good people.

However, you shouldn't do the same for the bad employees or, at least, not more than once. This would just allow them to continue to shift the monkey. When such employees mess up, it's fine to say, "How are you going to handle this?" Remember, the goal is to treat everyone well, not equally. You treat a strong employee well by giving him or her a much-needed break. You treat a weak employee well by building that person's capacity to make decisions and solve problems on his or her own.

Shouldering the responsibility for your good people is a way to build Tier Three leadership. It's much more effective than only taking care of yourself, while letting your good employees fend for themselves.

Give Good People a Break

You can also win points with your good employees by taking on annoying problems once in a while and shifting them to others. Suppose you're managing a restaurant one night, and you see an unwelcome sight: the arrival of a certain party of six people who come by occasionally and are impossible to satisfy. They complain about everything, give the waiter a rough time, and leave a lousy tip. These folks are

normally given to the very best waiter, who is best
equipped to put up with them, but once in a while
you deliberately have them seated in your worst
waiter's area. The great waiter who is normally stuck
with them will notice this and understand that you're
paying him back for his good work. You are also
showing the worst waiter that his poor performance
can't shield him from taking on tough problems.
You've redistributed monkeys to ensure the same
person isn't carrying them all the time.

Redistribute monkeys to ensure the same
person isn't carrying them all the time.

Similarly, if you're running a customer complaint
department, you would normally give the most
obnoxious customers to your best customer service
rep, because she can calm them down and placate
them. But every once in a while when you see a
particularly irate customer approaching, you can say
to her, "I'll take this one." She'll appreciate the break.

Show Your Strength

Taking a hit for your good employees and rewarding them with thanks, breaks, and anything else you
can offer will help them build monkey resistance. It's
also helpful to let them see that you are a strong leader
they can rely on and trust.

Effectively dealing with bad employees is a major
component of strong leadership. Handling distasteful
chores like firing ineffectual workers, while making

it clear that you made the decision and carried it out personally, will also show your leadership strength.

> Let employees see that you are a strong leader they can rely on and trust.

Weaker managers typically rely on their superiors to handle firing. They think this will allow them to remain friendly with the remaining employees, saying, "Hey, it was the general manager's decision, not mine." A strong leader takes the opposite approach, insisting on identifying and firing the slacker personally, even if the general manager has offered to do it. When you execute these difficult tasks personally, everyone knows that *you* are in charge. The good workers will see your strength and like it; the bad ones will see your strength and dislike it. The good workers will realize that you are strong enough to protect them, and that's how it should be.

Always remember:

* Give your good people permission *not* to take on additional duties.

* Don't let your good workers become consumed with guilt and remorse when they err. If they don't know they made a mistake, gently lead them to discover it by themselves. There's no need to discipline them; they will move the earth to make sure it never happens again.

* Always ask your people to do what you won't, because they're best at doing the work and you're best at leading the work.

* It's OK to give preferential treatment to your superstars, as long as you also give everyone else an opportunity to improve and shine.

* Protect your good workers from envious peers.

* Let everyone see that you are a strong leader.

Chapter 7

What Monkeys Do You Shift?

As leaders, we must learn to identify the myriad of monkeys the slothful, uncaring folks gleefully shift to anyone they can convince, or force, to accept them. These include the Fear Monkey, Guilt Monkey, Anger Monkey, Extra-Work Monkey, Resentment Monkey, Concern Monkey, and so on. Having read through this book, you now realize there are an unlimited number and variety of monkeys, and you could identify many I haven't mentioned.

We want to avoid creating inappropriate monkeys, but as leaders we must often shift monkeys ourselves. Many of these responsibilities are doled out due to necessity; work needs to get done! Sometimes, however, unnecessary monkeys pop up because of the inappropriate approaches we've used to deal with poorly performing workers and difficult people in our lives.

When we understand how our own actions create monkeys, we can learn to avoid them and substitute more positive actions. But first we've got to realize what we're doing that's causing the problem. Here's my top-nine list of monkeys that all leaders need to learn to stop putting on others' backs.

> When we understand how our own actions create monkeys, we can learn to avoid them and substitute more positive actions.

The Blanket Monkey

We use the Blanket Monkey when we want to avoid dealing with someone directly—like the employee who never arrives at the meeting on time, or turns in sloppy paperwork, or doesn't turn it in at all. Instead of dealing with these people individually, we try to correct the problem by addressing an entire group and putting the monkey on everyone's back. A leader who uses Blanket Monkeys typically begins memos, emails, and meetings with something like "Some of you have not been turning in your reports on time" in hopes that the person he's been avoiding will get the message and self-correct his behavior.

This approach is almost always ineffective, and it dumps monkeys on the backs of everyone in the organization. The most responsible people in the room will wonder who messed up and worry it might be them, and everyone will pay for the leader's reluctance to face the miscreants by being on the receiving end of the lecture.

To avoid the Blanket Monkey — Rather than sending a message to an anonymous receiver via the blanket memo, deal directly with the problem person. Put the monkey on his back and his back only.

The Rule Monkey

The Rule Monkey, like the Blanket Monkey, is generally used when the leader does not want to deal with the problem person individually. Instead, the leader creates a new policy that makes more work for those who did nothing wrong. For example, a bank manager may have all employees fill out a customer interaction form for every customer they deal with for weeks on end, or require every server to ask every single customer if they want to supersize their order.

Leaders who use the Rule Monkey are under the impression that you can control a person's behavior with rules. They also like to discuss topics in the employee handbook, health and safety codes, and so on. Often when this kind of leader starts talking, employees surreptitiously roll their eyes and mimic his next words under their breath.

To avoid the Rule Monkey   Rather than issuing rules to the entire group designed to change the behavior of a few, deal with those few individually and directly.

The Avoidance Monkey

Leaders who use the Avoidance Monkey think they can manage without engaging in any potentially challenging situations. Their theory is, why tackle anything today that you can put off until tomorrow. This allows negative employees with strong personalities to become more and more powerful. Because the leader is afraid of the negative people, everyone else also becomes fearful of these people.

The result of the leader's inaction is that a lot of good people end up with Fear Monkeys on their backs, and both morale and output will suffer.

To avoid the Avoidance Monkey	Deal with problems now. Nip them in the bud while they are still manageable and have not rotted the entire organization.

The Yelling Monkey

The Yelling Monkey is used by leaders who deal with everyone and everything by force: by trying to be loud and obnoxious.

Let me rephrase that: they are not trying to be loud and obnoxious, they *are* loud and obnoxious. They believe that if they repeat an idea, value, or expectation loudly and often enough, everyone will simply go along with it. As a result, the responsible people in the group end up loaded with Yelling Monkeys. Believe me, they do not like it! The irresponsible ones, however, won't take on these monkeys because they don't listen and don't care.

To avoid the Yelling Monkey	Keep your emotions in check and your decibel level reasonable. Deal with problems logically, not emotionally.

The Blame Monkey

The Blame Monkey is used by leaders who operate as if nothing is ever their fault; all problems are laid at someone else's feet. They make an employee, a policy, or a supervisor serve as a scapegoat for their own ineffectiveness.

Leaders who use the Blame Monkey are similar to those who use the Avoidance Monkey, but instead of avoiding problem people, they avoid responsibility. When monkeys that are rightfully theirs come their way, they duck and let them land on someone else's back.

To avoid the Blame Monkey	Remember that leaders get to take credit for things that go right, but they also must accept responsibility for problems and failures. Some monkeys *do* belong to you—don't shift them to others.

The Crying Monkey

A close cousin to the Yelling Monkey, the Crying Monkey has a favorite weapon—tears. This monkey is used by those whose primary reaction to anything stressful is tearing up. Those who use the Crying Monkey (more often employees than leaders) cry at any sign of trouble or disapproval. Crying becomes a weapon that wards off criticism, pressure, and responsibility—and shifts problems to someone else's back. Crying Monkeys never emerge as the result of care and concern about others' problems. They only appear to push one's own problems away.

This tactic often works: tears automatically soften the stance of the person who's putting on the pressure. However, respect for the crier and his or her chances for advancement usually fly out the window. And, of course, somebody else has to take on the crier's monkeys.

Leaders who use the Crying Monkey may get some temporary results, but they really lose credibility over the long term and are seen as weak and ineffectual.

To avoid the Crying Monkey	Learn to control your emotions! The work environment, especially, is not the place for tears. You may need to take a good look at yourself to realize how manipulative and, ultimately, relationship-killing this technique is. Handle your own responsibilities, and stop trying to unload them on others: you're stronger than you think!

The Pouting Monkey

People who use the Pouting Monkey become aloof or withdrawn in a silent expression of resentment when they're upset about something. This passive-aggressive approach is designed to make others feel so guilty or uncomfortable that they give the pouter whatever he wants. It's just easier to give in than it is to endure the cold, rejecting attitude.

It's very difficult for sympathetic and caring people to avoid the Pouting Monkey. They tend to handle a few fairly well, but are eventually overwhelmed when someone uses the Pouting Monkey regularly. Pouting Monkeys can proliferate, because it is sometimes easier to avoid the person or give in to her demands than to deal with her as an adult.

A leader who uses the Pouting Monkey becomes so unattractive to his or her best employees that those employees don't want to interact with, learn from, or follow the leader.

To avoid the Pouting Monkey Keep your emotions in check and your decibel level reasonable. Deal with problems logically, not emotionally.

The Lying Monkey

Some people protect themselves by using the Lying Monkey. You'd think such people would be easy to recognize because they couldn't look you straight in the eye, but unfortunately, these folks have gotten very good at telling bold untruths. They have learned that their mistakes can be laid at the feet of others, that denying often gets them off the hook, and that they can usually cover up their shortcomings by making up excuses.

At the core is a person who really doesn't like responsibility, isn't committed to the job or being a team player, and wants to take the easy way out. Lying may not be the person's worst trait, but he lies on a regular basis. Everyone hates being lied to—whether that person is a leader or an employee, and regardless of the motivation behind the lie.

To avoid the Lying Monkey As a leader, always speak truthfully. You may not always be able to give everyone every piece of information, and you may not want to, but don't lie to your people. If you can't or don't want to divulge something, simply say, "I'm not at liberty to discuss that."

The Arguing Monkey

The Arguing Monkey is handed out by people who are great at arguing. They love to confront others, take exception to just about anything, and flat-out contradict others. In fact, they've probably already had a couple of hours of arguing practice before they came in to work.

Both leaders and employees have been known to use Arguing Monkeys. When someone points out something they've done wrong, Arguing Monkeys come right back at the "accuser." They fight to "prove" their innocence, attack the other person's shortcomings, or just keep arguing (usually in a very loud voice) until the other person gives up and walks away.

It never helps to engage such a person, because when he argues, he's in his comfort zone. In addition, those who see two people arguing may be unable to tell which one is the troublemaker—the employee or the leader.

To avoid the Arguing Monkey	Don't start arguments yourself, and don't engage with people who do. Control your own emotions, and with those who argue with you, either ignore them or become a broken record, telling them what they need to do and nothing more.

Monitor Your Monkeys

These are just nine of the many monkeys to avoid. You can probably think of people in your own life who use these and many others, but the greater challenge is to keep an eye on whether you are using them yourself, especially during stressful situations. Once you realize that these monkeys are used as weapons in order to deflect responsibility, you can learn to keep your cool and manage your emotions whenever you feel a monkey looming over your shoulder. And when people realize that you neither use these monkeys yourself nor tolerate them in others, they'll be much more likely to put away their own monkeys—for good.

Always remember:

* As a leader, learn to recognize your challenging people's go-to monkeys.

* Be aware that some people will use multiple monkeys.

* Make sure that you do not use these monkeys in your own personal approach.

Epilogue

Keeping Monkeys on Your Mind

There's a never-ending supply of lazy, uncaring, and poorly performing workers who will happily shift their monkeys to anyone and everyone they can. They don't care about their duties, coworkers, customers, or anything else. For them, getting out of doing work is the ultimate goal. You can tell they're very good at it, because the caring, hard-working people who surround them shoulder many of the responsibilities that should be carried by the liars, criers, and slackers.

It's up to you, the leader, to understand how this dynamic damages the good workers' morale and performance, chews up your own time and energy, alienates customers, and weakens your entire department, division, or organization. That's why you must constantly ask yourself three questions:

1. Where is the monkey?
2. Where should the monkey be?
3. How do I shift the monkey to its proper place?

In every conversation with your workers, every group meeting, every walk through the work area or any other encounter—even if it's just a routine email from one of your staff—ask yourself these three questions. With just a little bit of practice, you'll become an expert at recognizing those out-of-place monkeys and shifting them back where they belong. Soon you'll come to the end of a work week and suddenly realize that, for the first time in years, you don't have to come into the office during the weekend, or spend Saturday and Sunday catching up at home. Why? Because when you corral those monkeys, you make poor performers work, free up high performers to handle the really important tasks, and leave yourself more time to do your own job, which is managing.

> With just a little bit of practice, you'll become an expert at recognizing those out-of-place monkeys and shifting them back where they belong.

It's a wonderful new beginning for everyone—except the problem workers.

While you're looking for misplaced monkeys among staff, also keep asking yourself if your company is shifting the monkey to your customers. This happens a lot—sometimes deliberately and sometimes inadvertently.

For example, it used to be that when you called a company, you almost always spoke with a real person. Today you get a voicemail system that forces you to punch a lot of buttons and figure things out yourself—as in "Press 1 if you know the extension of the party you are seeking; Press 2 for a company directory." Just think about what happens when you call your credit card company. You have to punch in your sixteen-digit credit card number, your zip code or other identifying criteria, and maybe your phone number as well. Then you have to repeat it all out loud when a representative finally comes on the line! This provides a lot of protection for the credit card company, but it makes you, the customer, do a lot of work. Where does that put the monkey? On the customer's back. Is that where the monkey should be?

I can understand creating these hoops if people are trying to cancel their credit cards, as the company doesn't want to let them go, but if a company is trying to retain customers, or get new ones, it should be very careful about making its customers do its work. Leaders should constantly ask, "Who carries the burden of this policy or practice?" Some may finally be asking themselves this question, because some credit card companies are now trying to attract customers by announcing that when you call you'll get to talk to a real person. They're competing on the basis of *not* putting a monkey on the customer's back.

> Leaders should constantly ask, "Who carries the burden of the policy or practice?"

Sometimes the company-imposed monkey consists of making the customer notice and respond to something or be forced to pay more. I recently used a travel website to book an airplane ticket and didn't notice until it was too late that I had also purchased travel insurance. A little box asked if you wanted the insurance with "Yes" already selected. If you didn't want the insurance, you had to uncheck it. I'm sure a lot of people like me don't see it—and many of those who do are probably annoyed that they have to uncheck a box to avoid purchasing something they don't want. Thanks to this technique, the average customer spends more money. But how many customers refuse to return because they are angered by this tactic?

It's not just faceless machines that help companies shift monkeys to their customers' backs. If you've ever gone to a fast food restaurant, you've seen a technique called *suggested selling* in action. That's when the clerk tries to sell you a meal rather than an individual item by asking, "Which meal would you like?" before you've said a word. When you do give your order, no matter what it is, the clerk will ask, "Would you like to supersize that?" or "Would you like fries with that?" or something similar.

The idea behind suggested selling is to increase the amount of the average purchase, but it puts the responsibility on the customer to say no. While it's not a matter of right or wrong, there is a point at which certain customers tire of monkeys and realize that the only way to avoid them is to go elsewhere. There is no question that suggested selling works; the average amount the customer spends does indeed go up. The real question is, does the average number of customers go down?

And what about all those little booths set up in the malls—the ones with eager salespeople stepping out to show you their wares or spray perfume or cologne on you as you walk by? This puts a monkey on the backs of customers who don't like this kind of approach. They may end up avoiding the mall. And how are malls doing today?

There are those who say, "Well, none of this matters to me. I don't mind saying no to supersizing or having to uncheck a box." That's correct; it doesn't matter to *some* people. But you don't know who it does matter to, or how many walk away because they're sick of monkeys. The only thing you know for sure is that a bunch of customers just don't return.

Sometimes it makes sense to shift the monkey to the customer. There's always a risk in doing so, however, because things are now out of balance. If one of your competitors decides to put the customer first, you can be sure a lot of your customers will go there in order to avoid the monkey. That's why it pays for you to think about the ways customers interact with your company and to keep asking yourself:

1. Where is the monkey?
2. Where should the monkey be?
3. How do I shift the monkey to its proper place?

Monkeys are an inescapable part of business and the rest of life. You, as a leader at work, home, and elsewhere, can go a long way toward creating a more positive, productive environment by protecting the good people and making sure that everybody deals with their own monkeys, and only their own monkeys. Whether you're a newly minted supervisor or the CEO, if you're in any leadership position at all, you can make your corner of the world a better place.

About the Author

TODD WHITAKER is a professor of educational leadership at Indiana State University. One of the nation's leading authorities on employee motivation and leadership effectiveness, his message has resonated with over a million professionals around the world. He has written more than twenty books.

Working With Difficult & Resistant Staff
By John F. Eller and Sheila A. Eller
This book will help school leaders understand how to prevent and address negative staff behaviors to ensure positive school change.
BKF407

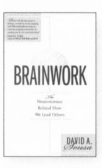

Brainwork
By David A. Sousa
Learn how to leverage the most provocative brain research to increase your productivity, expand your creative vision, and become a stronger leader.
BKN008

The Ball
By Todd Whitaker
Through this heartwarming parable, the author reminds you of the importance of keeping your focus and remaining true to yourself.
BKF611

Solution Tree | Press

a division of

Solution Tree

Visit solution-tree.com or call 800.733.6786 to order.